EFFECTIVE MANAGEMENT CONTROL:
CONTROL:
Theory and Practice

EFFECTIVE MANAGEMENT CONTROL:
Theory and Practice

by

Eric G. Flamholtz

Kluwer Academic Publishers
Boston/London/Dordrecht

Distributors for North America:
Kluwer Academic Publishers
101 Philip Drive
Assinippi Park
Norwell, Massachusetts 02061 USA

Distributors for all other countries:
Kluwer Academic Publishers Group
Distribution Centre
Post Office Box 322
3300 AH Dordrecht, THE NETHERLANDS

Library of Congress Cataloging-in-Publication Data

Flamholtz, Eric.
  Effective management control : theory and practice / Eric. G.
Flamholtz.
    p. cm.
  Includes bibliographical references and index.
  ISBN 0-7923-9699-5
  1. Organizational effectiveness. 2. Line and staff organization.
3. Compensation management. I. Title.
HD58.9.F588   1996
658-dc20   95-52283
                                        CIP

Printed on acid-free paper.

Printed in the United States of America

CONTENTS

FIGURES, TABLES AND EXHIBITS

PREFACE

This monograph deals with a critical but relatively neglected misunderstood aspect of organizational effectiveness: The process of controlling the behavior of people in organizations. Our overall purpose is to provide a framework to assist practicing managers as well as academics to understand the nature, role, features, and functioning of organizational control and control systems in organizations.

Control is an essential aspect of all organizational functioning. However, it is not as well understood as planning, leadership, or structural design. Although a great deal is written about the topic, we lack an integrated theory or set of techniques for facilitating effective control of organizations.

The basic objective of this study is to take some steps towards the development of a more comprehensive framework for understanding, designing, and managing control systems. The monograph is a hybrid of a treatise and a text and is intended for practicing managers as well as for students of management.

The monograph begins with a chapter dealing with the nature and role of organizational control. Chapter two presents a framework for understanding the nature of organizational control, and identifies the three principal parts of an organizational control system: 1) The core control system, 2) The organization's structure, and 3) The organization's culture. The core control system consists, in turn, of a series of "components": a planning sub-system, a measurement and feedback sub-system, an evaluation sub-system, and a reward sub-system.

Chapters three through six deal with each of these components of the core control system. Each examines the role of these components of a core control system as part of an overall organizational control system per se. Chapter seven examines the role of organizational structure and culture in control.

Chapter eight examines the role of the firm's accounting system as a control system. Accounting is often thought of as a control system but, as shown in this monograph, it can not function independently as a control system. It needs to be connected with other parts of the overall control system in order to function effectively as a control mechanism. Accordingly, chapter eight examines the extent to which accounting can function as a control system and what needs to be done in order to make it part of an effective system of organizational control.

In the final chapter of the monograph (chapter nine), we turn our attention to the issues involving the overall design of effective control systems in organizations. The design of an effective control system for an organization is a critical issue. If there is too little control, an organization can drift into chaos, and, in turn, fail. For example, Osborne Computers did not have an adequate control system over its finances and manufacturing costs and went bankrupt. On the contrary, if an organization develops an organizational control system with too great a degree of control, then innovation and entrepreneurship can be significantly suppressed. This has been the problem of a number of major organizational bureaucracies including: AT & T, IBM, and General Motors. Thus, the issue of organizational control and the design of an optimal control system is essential for long-term organizational effectiveness. The chapter presents a framework to facilitate the design and evaluation of control systems. It also presents some examples and a mini-case study to illustrate the practical issues involved.

This monograph is intended for a dual audience. It is intended for both practicing managers as well as students of the practice of management. Accordingly, it attempts to strike a balance between providing a relatively straight-forward and understandable text, together with certain conceptual or academic perspectives that are necessary both to the practicing manager as well as to the scholar. The balance between these two audiences is not always easy to reach, and the reader is asked to bear with the author in this respect. At times, the framework may be too "academic" for the practicing manager, while simultaneously it may be too "practical" for the research scholar. Wherever feasible, I have oriented text towards the practicing manager, with chapter endnotes being directed towards the research component of this audience. However, in certain instances, I have chosen to briefly summarize selected research studies which I think are of particular relevance to the practicing manager. Similarly, certain portions of the monograph are necessarily technical in nature. In order to fulfill its objective of providing a comprehensive framework that can be used by practicing managers, I have chosen to summarize certain technical information, especially with respect to evaluation systems, that is also treated in certain texts. The basic rationale is that I wanted this monograph to be a "stand alone managerial tool" for all those who might chose to use it.

In brief, I hope that the practicing manager will pardon me when the discussion becomes too academic or theoretical, and that the research scholar will pardon me when the discussion becomes too much like a text for the practicing manager. Taken as a whole, I believe that both audiences will find value in the monograph.

The bottom line is that the monograph's intent is to contribute to our understanding of how to achieve the optimal degree of control in organizations by designing and using control systems as an effective managerial tool. To accomplish this, we need to understand what control is, what a control system is, how the key components of a control system function, and how to design, manage, and redesign actual organizational control systems. This monograph provides a conceptual framework to facilitate this understanding. This framework should be useful to academics by providing an integrated approach to control systems issues and problems. It should be useful to practicing managers by providing a lens through which to analyze control systems in their own organizations.

THE NATURE AND ROLE OF ORGANIZATIONAL CONTROL

All organizations (businesses, universities, governments, hospitals) are concerned with channeling human efforts toward attainment of organizational objectives. Regardless of their formal purposes, organizations are composed of people with their own personal interests. Even if these individuals and groups wish to help attain organizational goals, the organization of which they are a part must coordinate their efforts and direct them toward specific goals. Thus organizations must influence or control the behavior of people, if they are to fulfill their plans and achieve their goals.

To help gain control over the behavior of people in formal organizations, most enterprises use a combination of techniques including personal supervision, rules, standard operating procedures, job descriptions, budgets, accounting measurements, and performance appraisal systems. Taken together, these techniques are part of an invisible yet very real system: The organizational control system.

Control plays a major part in the management of an enterprise, but unlike machines, equipment, finances, and people its role is often hidden from view. When we examine an organization's structure, we see it in the form of an "organizational chart." Unfortunately, there is nothing like this to help us visualize an organization's control systems. Thus organizational control and organizational control systems are ubiquitous but difficult to visualize; they are pervasive yet tenuous; they are invisible, but have a significant impact on people's behavior.

Although control is a critical component of any system (human or mechanical), the area of management control has been relatively less developed than other management processes. Specifically, we lack an integrated conceptual framework to understand, visualize, and analyze control issues.

This book deals with organizational control: its nature, role, functioning, and effects. It develops the concept of control as well as the notion of a control system. It also considers the relation between control and human behavior in organizations. It examines the elements of an organizational control system as well as the process of designing such systems. The basic purpose of this book is to examine this relatively neglected but indispensable aspect of management, and show how organizational control systems can play an important role as a component of the overall management process.

We shall focus upon some key issues concerning organizational control:

1. What is the nature of control in organizations?

2. Why are organizational control and organizational control systems necessary for effective organizational performance?

3. What is an organizational control system and how does it function to influence human behavior in organizations?

4. How do accounting and budgeting systems function to influence human behavior as components of an overall organizational control system?

5. How can (and should) organizations design control systems which influence behavior in desired ways?

The remainder of this chapter shall focus upon the first question above, while the other issues will be examined in subsequent chapters.

THE NATURE OF CONTROL

The term "control" is typically used in a variety of ways.[1] In this book, our concern is with organizational control, which is the process of controlling or influencing the behavior of people as members of a formal organization to increase the likelihood that they will achieve organizational goals.[2]

There are four critical dimension of this concept of control: 1) it is oriented to goals; 2) it relates to a lack of goal congruence; 3) it refers to a process; and 4) it is probabilistic. These features shall be examined in turn.

Goal Orientation of Control

The concept of control used here is based upon the idea that the purpose or raison d'etre of control is to assist the organization in achieving its "goals." As used here, the term "goals" refers to those things which the organizational seeks to attain.[3] An organization's goals may be the goal's of an individual entrepreneur or CEO; they may be the goals of a committee or set of committees. There may even be goals that are not chosen by the organization, but merely imposed upon it by an external group or authority. Regardless of the source of its goals, all control systems must be goal-oriented.

Lack of Total Goal Congruence

We also assume that the goals of the organization are not necessarily the same goals of all of the entity's individual or group members. The larger the organization, the less likely the goals of all of its members are to be congruent. For an organization to function effectively, it would be ideal if all members shared the same goals. This idealized state of total goal congruence, or an identity between the goals of all organization members and the organization as a whole, is shown in Figure 1-1. Unfortunately, the state of total goal congruence is rarely, if ever, attained, except perhaps in a one-person firm where the owner is the only employee. More typically, there is a partial sharing of goals between organizational members and the entity. This is shown schematically in Figure 1-2. The amount or area of congruence is represented by cross-hatching.

Control is a Process

This concept of control views it as an ongoing process. Control is dynamic and not static. It must adjust to changes in goals over time.

Although there are techniques of control, they are merely components of the control process which is intended to increase the degree of goal congruence.

Control is Probabilistic

From a practical perspective, the aim of a control system is to maximize the likelihood that people will behave in ways which are consistent with organizational objectives. No system can guarantee that this will occur all of the time. This means that control is probabilistic rather than deterministic.

In summary, organizational control is a process which is designed: 1) to motivate people to achieve goals, and 2) to influence the probability that people will behave in the desired ways. It can not guarantee, nor does it intend to, control one-hundred percent of peoples' behavior.

Connotative and Denotative Meanings of Control

Words have both connotative an denotative meanings. For example, a ""frog" is a small aquatic animal. This is a denotative definition. But "frogs" connote: "Warts, croaking, and slime." The denotative meaning is neutral and none valuative. Connotative meanings may be positive or negative and are evaluative.

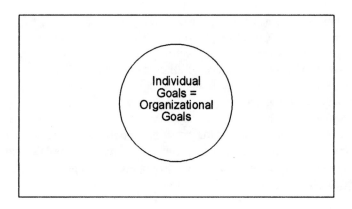

Figure 1-1
Schematic of Total Goal Congruence

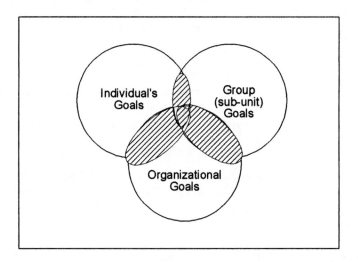

Figure 1-2
Schematic of Partial Goal Congruence

For some, the connotative meaning of control is positive. It suggests an idea of "being in control," a sense of order. For others, the notion of control has negative connotations. It implies that people are controlled or manipulated.

As we shall see, control is a tool, like hammer or a computer, and it is required for effective organizational performance. At this point, it should be merely noted that the concept of control is not merely technical, but has psychological overtones as well.

THE NEED FOR ORGANIZATIONAL CONTROL

Why do organizations require control? Organizations require control because they consist of people with different interests, different tasks, and different perspectives. The efforts of people require coordination and direction and this, in turn creates the need for control.

The larger the number of people in an organization, the greater the need for some form of organizational control mechanism. In relatively small entrepreneurial organizations, "control" is experienced by the entrepreneur who can see what is happening on a day-to-day basis and make personal interventions. In large, complex enterprises, such as IBM, AT&T, and General Motors, more complex, formal mechanisms of control must be designed and used. However, these formal control systems must be designed with care in order to achieve the optimal degree of control; one which is neither too loose (which may lead to chaos), or too tight (which may lead to stifling bureaucracy).

Functions of Control

In order to motivate people to behave in ways consistent with organizational goals, control systems must perform three related tasks. First, they must be able to motivate people to make decisions and take actions which are consistent with organizational objectives. Without control systems, people take actions or make decisions designed to fulfill their own needs rather than the organization's goals. For example, the organization may be concerned with cost control while an individual is tempted to travel first-class.

Next, control systems must coordinate the efforts of several different parts of an organization. Even when people are trying to act in the organizations' best interests, they may find themselves working at cross-purposes. For example, a sales unit may want to offer a customer expedited delivery to make a sale, while from manufacturing's perspective, this may mean a "rush order" which disrupts carefully designed production schedules and causes inefficiency.

The third task of a control system is to provide information about the results of operation, and people's performance. This information allows the organization to evaluate results, while simultaneously permitting people to operate on a daily basis without having every decision reviewed. This is referred to as, "autonomy with control." To illustrate this, we shall examine selected situations in which goal congruence may be lacking, which, thus, indicates the need for control.

Focus on Goals

In all organizations, people must be motivated to focus on organizational goals. On a daily basis, people make decisions which may or may not be consistent with organizational goals. Ideally, the control system will cause people to on achieving the goals of the organization. This creates a state of "goal consequence," described above.

Coordination

In all organizations, there is a need to coordinate the efforts of people. Even in relatively small forms, those with sales of less than $1 million, problems may be caused by a lack of coordination.

It is useful to think of an organization such as a business as a "human machine." The parts of this machine must articulate or else they may tend to move or work at cross-purposes. In some situations, the control process may consist merely of a series of meetings and periodic opportunity to assess progress against those goals by oral or written reports. Carefully designed, this may be an adequate "control system" for certain types and sizes of organizations.

In larger, more complex organizations, the problem of coordination may be much more than trivial. In firms such as General Electric with several different businesses, operating in several different nations, the effort required simply for coordination may be quite substantial.

Autonomy with Control

Another reason for control systems is to permit the decentralization of day to day operations while simultaneously assuring that organizational objectives are achieved. This need has been recognized since the early portion of the twentieth century. A classic example of this purpose of control is described by Alfred P. Sloan as part of his experience in managing General Motors as a national corporation during the 1930s. Sloan stated that the firm had established techniques of control over individual matters such as cost, inventory and production, but the fundamental issue of how to achieve optimal control remained:

> How could we exercise permanent control over the whole corporation in a way consistent with the decentralized scheme of the organization?... The means, as it turned out, was a method of financial control which converted the

broad principle of return on investment into one of the important working instruments for measuring the operations of the divisions.[4]

The basic strategy was to permit managers to run their day to day operations as they wished, while evaluating the results of their decisions and actions in terms of the criterion of rate of return on investment. This permitted managers a great deal of autonomy, while still allowing top management to control the goals of the operating executives. It thus optimized, rather than either maximized or minimized, the degree of control.

The issue of how to optimize control (that is, to simultaneously permit managers sufficient autonomy while maintaining overall control) is of widespread significance. Historically, some firms such as ITT (International Telephone and Telegraph) under the leadership of Harold Geneen resolved it by developing highly centralized control systems, while others equally large firms (such as Beatrice Foods under William Karnes) are able to run $8 billion organizations with a staff of 100 people or less.

Implementation of Planning

Another function of control systems is to facilitate the implementation of planning and the planning process. Many organizations mistakenly believe that planning is complete when a written plan has been developed. Unfortunately, this is merely the end of the beginning, and an effective control system is required if plans are to be fulfilled. Another way to look at this is that planning is actually a component of a control process, and not a stand-alone system, per se. We shall develop this point further in chapter two.

CONTROL VERSUS CONTROL SYSTEMS

Control over an organization can be exercised through many mediums. A manager can exercise control by means of his or her personal supervision, leadership and involvement in day to day activities. Techniques such as job descriptions, rules and standard operating procedures can also be used. Budgets, performance appraisal systems, and incentive compensation plans are also commonly employed in attempts to control behavior.

Taken together, we might wish to call all of these things a "control system." Yet as we shall see in Chapter 2, the mere existence of an ad hoc collection of techniques control does not comprise a true control system.

Nature of a Control System

An "organizational control system" may be defined as a set of mechanisms--both processes and techniques--which are designed to increase the probability that people will behave in ways that lead to the attainment of organizational objectives. The ultimate objective of a control system is not to control the specific behavior of people per se, but, rather, to influence people to take actions and make decisions which in their judgement are consistent with organizational goals.[5]

Different Methods of Control

How does control differ from control systems? Control is a generic process. It can be exercised either by: 1) supervision, 2) leadership, 3) an ad hoc collection of control mechanisms which have not been designed explicitly to articulate with one another for the purpose of control, as shown in Figure 1-3.

	Personal Control	**Impersonal Control**
PLANNED	2 Leadership	4 Formal Control System
UNPLANNED	1 Ad Hoc Supervision	3 Ad Hoc Techniques

Figure 1-3
Typology of Control

Supervision as a Method of Control

The process of supervision refers to the day to day scheduling, observation, and oversight of work. We use the term supervision if the process through which this occurs is ad hoc or intermittent rather than planned.

Supervision typically occurs as a by-product of managerial activity. During the course of day to day interactions between managers and staff, work is assigned, observed, reviewed and suggestions are made. Regularly scheduled staff meetings are unlikely to occur. The work planning process is typically informal, and explicit goals or standards are not likely to be set. In addition, performance appraisal is likely to be casual and intermittent rather than regularly scheduled and part of a formal process.

The "supervisory method of control," just described, is quite common. It is most typical of relatively small firms, with sales less than $5 million. Yet it can be observed in multi-billion dollar enterprises at all levels of management.

Although it may not be thought of as a method of control as such by the managers who practice it, nevertheless the ad hoc supervisory method is an implicit control strategy. It is shown in Figure 1-3 as an unplanned method of personal control.

Leadership as a Method of Control

The process of leadership refers to the use of formal (appointed) leaders to perform several responsibilities in order to influence the behavior of people to achieve organizational goals. Just as supervision, leadership is a personal method of control.

Leadership differs from supervision in that there are an explicit, predefined set of processes which leaders are expected to use to influence the behavior of people who are their subordinates. The leader is expected to set performance goals, help facilitate work, stimulate group interaction and communications as well as to provide performance feedback, personal support and recognition. These are just some of the most common leadership functions.

There are many different theories of leadership, which prescribe what functions leaders should perform and how these functions ought to be performed.[6] In brief, leadership is a planned method of personal control.

Ad Hoc Control Techniques as a Method of Control

Some of the most common techniques of control have been noted above: job descriptions, rules, standard operating procedures, appraisal systems, budgets, etc. It is very common for such techniques to be used in organizations on a piecemeal basis. They are typically added one-at-a-time as the organization grows and experiences greater need for control.

Although this is a realistic and practical way to increase control, the principal disadvantage of the ad hoc method of control is that the   collection of control techniques used have not been designed as a system. Thus individual techniques may actually work at cross-purposes; or, even more significantly, important aspects of organizational performance may not be adequately controlled. For example, one of the current problems facing U.S. automotive companies is a comparative disadvantage in product quality vis a vis Japanese and West German companies. Automobiles produced by Japanese and West German companies are perceived by the U.S.

consumers as superior in terms of certain aspects of product quality, i.e., "fits and finishes."   U.S. automotive companies have always had systems for quality control and inspections. Nevertheless, the overall control system does not appear to have placed sufficient emphasis upon quality to satisfy consumer tastes and preferences. It is possible that the quality control systems used by automotive companies worked at cross purposed with the firm's unwritten control system: its culture. An automobile worker at one major company described the changing philosophy as follows:

> We used to be told: "if you can get it to run out the door, we can sell it." But now we know that that's bad business in the long run. Today, everything is quality, quality, quality.

Thus, in this example, it is clear that historically inadequate control was exercised over product quality. However, it is not clear whether the problem was that the quality control techniques were working at cross-purposes with the firm's culture, whether the control mechanisms were simply not functioning, or whether the control techniques were actually operating in accord with the company's objectives.

In brief, control techniques are an unplanned method of impersonal control. The term "impersonal control" is used to refer to control by means of systems and procedures rather than through personal efforts.

Formal Control System as a Method of Control

The term control system has been defined above. It refers to a set of processes and techniques which have been designed explicitly as a system to influence the behavior of people. It is a planned method of impersonal control.

Organizational Requirements for Control Systems

All organizations need control; but not all organizations require control systems. The four different methods of control are each appropriate under different circumstances, or stages of an organization's development.[7] We can identify or define four stages of organizational growth, at which, different methods of control are appropriate.

Stage I. In relatively small organizations, ad hoc supervision may be quite effective. In the course of daily operations, managers may be able to provide sufficient input to permit people to function smoothly without the need for formal goal setting, meetings, reports, etc. However, at some stage of development, an organization may reach a size that exceeds the capacity for informal, ad hoc supervision. Stage I generally characterizes firms with less than $5 million in sales.

Stage II. The next stage typically requires more formal leadership and certain control techniques. Formal goal setting sessions, regular staff meetings, reports, budgets, policies and similar techniques will be of assistance in increasing controls. This typically occurs during period of rapid growth, and typically characterizes firms with sales from $5-50 million.

Stage III. Once a firm has sales in excess of $50 million, it is increasingly difficult to achieve effective control without a formal control system. Of course, there are many examples of successful of even much greater size which do not have well designed, effectively functioning control systems. Those firms do, however, pay a price for the lack of such systems. The price may be concealed, and exist only as an opportunity cost. Nevertheless, it is real.

Stage IV. In large, multi-billion dollar enterprises, the control systems required may be quite complex, and component parts may not set well with each other. In some instances, the cost of an inadequate control system can be very great and only observed in a catastrophic situation. For example, a large well-known firm that suddenly incurs huge losses and finds itself out of control after years of profitability and benevolent neglect. The costs of ineffective control can be hidden by other positive factors, and may reveal themselves only after deterioration in other areas.

In brief, all organizations do not require the same method of control. The specific method of required control depends upon the stage of development of a firm and especially its size. The larger the firm, the greater the need for planned and formal methods of control. Similarly, within organizations the smaller the unit to be controlled, the less the need for planned, formal methods.

CONCLUSION

This chapter has examined the nature and role of organizational control. It has also identified different methods of control, and distinguished between control and a control system.[8]

Except for very small organizations, the need for control is ubiquitous. All organizations require control systems. These systems may be difficult to visualize, but they are real nonetheless. In chapter two, we shall provide a framework that helps make an "invisible" control system more tangible.

ENDNOTES

1. The literature on control is quite diverse, but can be categorized as comprising three different perspectives: the sociological, the administrative, and the psychological. For a review of the academic literature from these three perspectives, see Flamholtz, Das, and Tsui (1985). Also see K.A. Merchant, Control in Business Organizations, Boston, Pitman Publishing, Inc., 1985.

2. For alternative conceptualizations of control, see: Weber (1947), Thompson (1967), Perrow (1977), Ouchi (1977); Birnberg and Snodgrass (1988); Gupta and Govindarajan (1991).

3. Empirical research on the relationship of goals and performance standards as components of a control system may be found in the organizational psychology literature (Ivancevich, 1976, 1977; Kim and Hammer, 1976; Latham and Yuki, 1975; Locke, 1968; Terborg, 1976; Matsui et al, 1987; Mitchell and Silver, 1990; Kernan and Lord, 1990; Wright, 1990; Weingart, 1992; Meyer and Gettatly, 1988; Earley et al., 1989; Gettatly and Meyer, 1992).

4. Alfred P. Sloan, My Years With General Motors, New York: MacFadden-Bartell, 1965.

5. This is a constitutive or conceptual definition of an organizational control system. In Chapter 2, we shall define a control system in operational terms; that is, in terms of the operational subsystems which comprise the process and mechanisms of control.

6. For further discussion of leadership theories, see for example B.M. Bass, Leadership and Performance Beyond Expectations, (New York: Free Press, 1985); W. Bennis and B. Nanus, Leaders, (New York: Harper & Row, 1985); J.A. Conger, The Charismatic Leader, (San Francisco: Jossey-Bass, 1989); J.P. Kotter, The Leadership Factor, (New York: Free Press, 1988); H. Mintzberg, The Nature of Managerial Work, (New York: Harper & Row, 1973); Bennis, On Becoming a Leader, (Reading Mass., Addison-Wesley, 1989); and T.J. Peters and R.H. Waterman Jr., In Search of Excellence, (New York: Harper & Row, 1982); R.P. Vecchio, "Situational Leadership Theory: An Examination of a Prescriptive Theory", Journal of Applied Psychology, 1987, 72,3,444-451; Kozlowki and M.L. Doherty, "Integration of Climate and Leadership: Examination of a Neglected Issue", Journal of Applied Psychology, 1989, 74:4,546-553.

7. For further discussion of the stages of organizational growth as well as the nature of control required at each stage, see E.G. Flamholtz, Growing Pains: How to Make The Transition From Entrepreneurship to a Professionally Managed Firm, (San Francisco, CA: Jossey-Bass Publishers, Inc., 1990). It should be noted that the four stages of organizational control systems described her differ from those described in Growing Pains... to some extent.

8. This chapter constitutes a behaviorally based approach to organizational control. For other approaches, see Eisenhardt, K.M., "Control: Organizational and Economic Approaches," Management Science, Vol. 31, pp. 134-149 (1985); Williamson, D.E., The Economic Institutions of Capitalism, New York: Free Press, 1985; and Egelhoff, W.G., "Organizing The Multinational Enterprise: An Information Processing Perspective," Cambridge, MA: Ballinger, 1988.

REFERENCES

Argryis, C. "The Dilemma of Implementing Controls: The Case of Managerial Accounting," Accounting, Organizations, and Society, 1990:15:6, 503-512.

Bass, B.M., Leadership and Performance Beyond Expectations, New York: Free Press, 1985.

Bennis, W. On Becoming A Leader, Reading, Mass., Addison-Wesley, 1989.

Bennis, W. and Nanus, B., Leaders, New York: Harper & Row, 1985.

Birnberg, J.G. and Snodgrass, C., "Culture and Control: A Field Study," Accounting, Organizations and Society, Vol. 13, No. 5, 1988, pp. 447-464.

Conger, J.A., "The Charismatic Leader," San Francisco, CA: Jossey-Bass, 1989.

Daley, I., James, J., Sundem, G., Kondo, Y. "Attitudes Toward Final Control Systems in the United States and Japan", Journal of International Business Studies, 1985, 3:91-110.

Dermer, J., "Control and Organizational Order", Accounting, Organizations and Society, 1988, 13:1; 25-36.

Earley, P.C., P. Wojnaroski, and W. Prest, "Task Planning and Energy Expended: Exploration of How Goals Influence Performance", Journal of Applied Psychology, 72,1,107-114.

Egelhoff, W.G., Organizing the Multinational Enterprise: An Information-Processing Perspective, Cambridge, MA: Ballinger, 1988.

Eisenhardt, K.M., "Control: Organizational and Economic Approaches," Management Science, Vol. 31, 1985, pp. 134-149.

Erez, M., Earley, C. and C.L. Hulin, "The Impact of Participation of Goal Acceptance and Performance: A Two Step Model", Academy of Management Journal, 1985,28:1, 50-66.

Ezzamel, M. and M. Bourn, "The Role of Accounting Information Systems in an Organization Experiencing Financial Crisis," Accounting, Organizations and Society, 1990,26:5, 399-242.

Flamholtz, E.G., Das, T.K., and Tsui, A.S., "Toward an Integrative Framework of Organizational Control," Accounting, Organizations and Society, Vol. 10, No. 1, 1985, pp. 35-50.

Flamholtz, E.G., Growing Pains: How to Make the Transition from an Entrepreneurship to a Professionally Managed Firm, San Francisco, CA: Jossey-Bass Publishers, Inc., 1990.

Gellatly, I.R. and J.P. Meyer,"The Effects of Goal Difficulty on Physiological Arousal, Cognition, and Task Performance", Journal of Applied Psychology, 1992, 77:5,694-703.

Gerlinger, J. and Herbert L. "Control and Performance in International Joint Ventures", Journal of International Business Studies, 1990,2:235-254.

Govindarajan, V. and Gupta, A.K., "Linking Control Systems to Business Unit Strategy: Impact on Performance," Accounting, Organizations and Society, Vol. 10, No. 1, 1985, pp. 51-66.

Gupta, A.K. and Govindarajan, V., "Knowledge Flows and The Structure of Control Within Multinational Corporations," The Academy of Management Review, Vol. 16, No. 4, October, 1991, pp. 768-779.

Harpax, I., "Importance of Work Goals: An International Perspective," Journal of International Business Studies, 1990, 1:75-93.

Ivancevich, J., "Effects of Goal Setting on Performance and Job Satisfaction," Journal of Applied Psychology, 1976, pp. 605-612.

Ivancevich, J., "Different Goal Setting Treatments And their Effects on Performance and Job Satisfaction," Journal of Applied Psychology, 1977, pp. 406-419.

Kernan, M.C., and R.G. Lord, "Effects of Valence, Expectancies, and Goal-Performance Discrepancies in Single and Multiple Goal Environments", Journal of Applied Psychology, 1990, 75:2,194-203.

Kim, J. and Hamner, W., "The Effects of Performance Feedback and Goal Setting on Productivity and Satisfaction in an Organizational Setting," Journal of Applied Psychology, 1976, pp. 48-57.

Kotter, J.P., The Leadership Factor, New York: Free Press, 1988.

Kotter, J.P. and J.L Heskett, Corporate Culture and Performance, New York, Free Press, 1992.

Kozlowski, G. and M.L. Doherty, "Integration of Climate and Leadership: Examination of a Neglected Issue, Journal of Applied Psychology, 1989,74:4,546-553.

Latham, G.P. and Yukl, G.A., "A Review of Research in The Application of Goal Setting in Organizations," Academy of Management Journal, 1975, pp. 824-845.

Laughlin, R. "Accounting Systems in Organizational Contexts: A Critical Theory". Accounting,

Organizations and Society, 1987, 0.:5,479-512.

Locke, E.A., "Towards a Theory of Task Motivation and Incentives," Organizational Behavior and Human Performance, 1968, pp. 157-189.

Martinez, J.I. and Jarillo, J.C., "The Evolution of Research on Coordination Mechanisms in Multinational Corporations," Journal of International Business Studies, Vol. 20, 1989, pp. 489-514.

Matsui, T., Kakuyama, T., and Ongatco, "Effects of Goals and Feedback on Performance in Groups", Journal of Applied Psychology, 1987, &2:3,407-415.

Merchant, K.A., Control in Business Organizations, Boston: Pitman Publishing, Inc., 1985.

Merchant, K. "The Effects of Financial Controls on Data Manipulation and Management Myopia", Accounting, Organizations and Society, 1990, 15:4, 297-314.

Meyer, J.P. and Gellatly, I.R., "Perceived Performance Norm as a Mediator in the Effect of Assigned Goal on Personal Goal and Task Performance", Journal of Applied Psychology, 1988, 73:3,410-420.

Mintzberg, H., The Nature of Managerial Work, New York: Harper & Row, 1973.

Mitchell, T.R. and W.S. Silver, "Individual and Group Goals When Workers Are Interdependent: Effects on Task Strategies and Performance", Journal of Applied Psychology, 1990, 75:2, 185-193.

Norburn, D., Birley, S., Payne, A., and Dunn, M., "A Four Nation Study of the Relationship between Marketing Effectiveness, Corporate Culture, Corporate Values and Market Orientation", Journal of International Business Studies, 1990, 3: 451-468.

Ouchi, W.G., "The Relationship Between Organizational Structure and Organizational Control," Administrative Science Quarterly, Vol. 22, 1977, pp. 95-113.

Ouchi, W.G. and McGujire, M., "Organizational Control: Two Functions," Administrative Science Quarterly, Vol. 20, 1975, pp. 559-569.

Perrow, C., "The Bureaucratic Paradox: The Efficient Organization Centralizes in Order to Decentralize," Organizational Dynamics, 1977, pp. 3-14.

Peters, T.J. and Waterman Jr., R.H., In Search of Excellence, New York: Harper & Row, 1982.

Sloan, A.P., My Years at General Motors. New York: MacFadden-Bartell, 1965.

Terborg, J., "The Motivational Components of Goal Setting," Journal of Applied Psychology, 1976, pp. 613-621.

Thompson, J.D., Organizations In Action, New York: McGraw-Hill, 1967.

Vecchio, R.P., "Situational Leadership Theory: An Examination of a Prescriptive Theory," Journal of Applied Psychology, 1987, 72,3, 444-451.

Walsh, J. and J. Seward, "On the Efficiency of Internal and External Corporate Control Mechanisms", Academy of Management Review, 1990; 15:3, 421-458.

Weber, M., The Theory of Social and Economic Organization, (translated by Henderson, A.M. and Parsons, T.), New York: Free Press, 1947.

Weingart, L.R., "Impact of Group Goals, Task Component Complexity, Effort and Planning on Group Performance", Journal of Applied Psychology, 1992: 77:5 682-693.

Williamson, O.E., The Economic Institutions of Capitalism, New York: Free Press, 1985.

Wright,P.M., "Operationalization of Goal Difficulty as a Moderator of the Goal Difficulty-Performance Relationship", Journal of Applied Psychology, 1990, 75:3, 227-234.

2

ORGANIZATIONAL CONTROL
SYSTEMS: A FRAMEWORK

Organizational control systems (or, for brevity, "Control Systems") are not visible to the naked eyes of observers in an organization. Yet they are not metaphysical; they are real and permeate an organization.

Control systems are not easily seen or perceived by observers because they comprise a complex set of on-going organizational processes: the budgeting process, strategic planning, measurement and performance evaluation, the compensation system, and so on.

Since control systems are of fundamental importance to organizations, we need some way of making them more tangible. To make them easier to grasp, this chapter presents a generic model of an organizational control system.[9] It specifies the major components of a control system, describes them, and examines how they ought to be articulated if effective control is to be achieved in operating organizations.

This model can be used as a framework for both describing an organizations' control system as well as to evaluate its functioning and effectiveness. Once we have presented the framework, we shall illustrate its practical application by describing and evaluating an actual control system of a medium-sized residential real estate firm.

A MODEL OF AN ORGANIZATIONAL CONTROL SYSTEM

The model of an organizational control system presented here is represented schematically in Figure 2-1 as a set of concentric circles.[10] The model consists of three parts:

1. a "core control system",
2. organizational structure, and
3. organizational culture.

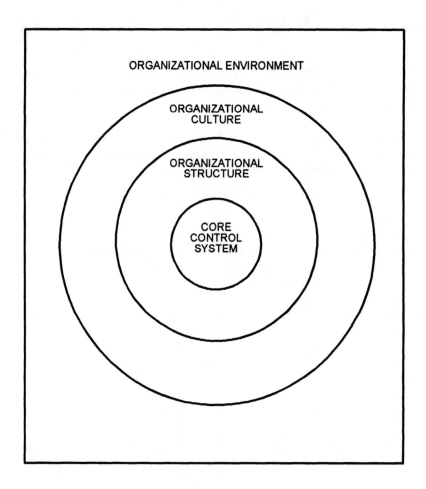

Figure 2-1
Schematic Representation of an Organizational Control System

The innermost circle comprises the "core control system." This is a cybernetic structure consisting of four subsystems (planning, operations, measurement, and evaluation-reward) which are articulated (linked) by feedback and feed-forward loops. The middle circle comprises the organization's structure: its set of rules and their interrelationships. The outer circle represents the organization's culture: its value system, beliefs, assumptions; the patterned ways of thinking which are characteristic of the entity. Those three elements of the control system are bounded by the organization's environment. We shall examine each part of a control system, beginning with the core control system.

The Core Control System

Although the applicability of cybernetic concepts to organizational control has been challenged, the main problem has been the narrow interpretation of mathematical cybernetics and the use of mechanistic analogies (i.e., the thermostat model of control).[11] However, the concept of the core control system presented here presents and integrated structure of five basic organizational processes: planning, operations, measurement, feedback and evaluation-reward. The core model is presented schematically in figure 2-2.

The Planning Subsystem

Planning, which can itself be defined in many ways, is basically the process of deciding about the objectives and goals of an organization (and/or its members) as well as the means to attain those objectives goals.[12] "Organizational goals," according to Hall "are the desired ends or states of affairs for whose achievement system policies are committed and resources allocated."[13] In this context, the term "objectives" refers to relatively broad statements about things an organization wishes to achieve in a given "performance area" (markets, products, personnel, financial results, etc.). "Goals" represent the quantitative level of aspiration sought to be attained for a given objective. For example, the financial objective for Pepsico may be "to earn a satisfactory return upon net assets employed in the business," while its goal or standard of performance for a given year might be "18% pretax ROI." The role of the planning subsystem in control is considered further in chapter 3.

The Operational Subsystem

Operations, or the operational subsystem refers to the on-going system for performing the functions required for day-to-day organizational activities. These are the responsibilities and activities specified in organizational roles.

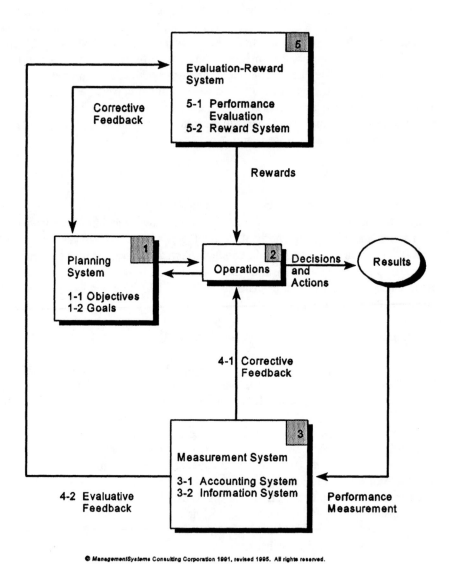

Figure 2-2
Schematic Model of The Core Control System

The Measurement Subsystem

In an organizational context, measurement is the process of assigning numbers to represent aspects of organizational behavior and performance.   The overall measurement system includes the accounting system with its measures of financial and managerial performance.   It also includes nonfinancial measures of organizational performance, including production indices such as scrap rates, capacity utilization and product quality (rejection ratios) measures as well as (at least potentially) social accountability measurements.

Measurement performs a dual function as part of a control system.   One function is that numbers generated may be used to monitor the extent to which goals and standards have been achieved, so that organizational members may be provided corrective and/or evaluative feedback.   This is termed the "output function" of measurement.   The second function of measurement related not to the numbers produced by measurement operations, but rather to the phenomena caused by the <u>act</u> or <u>process</u> of measurement <u>per se</u>.   The very fact that something is the subject of measurement tends to influence the behavior of people in organizations.[14]   Thus the medium of measurement itself a stimulus.   This is termed the "process function" of measurement.   The role of measurement in control is examined in more depth in Chapter four.

The accounting system is a component of the measurement system of an overall control system.   The budgeting system in organizations is part of the planning system as well as the measurement system.   However, <u>neither the accounting nor the budgetary system are equivalent to the whole of a control system</u>, because they lack critical components.   In the case of the accounting system the pieces missing are planning and evaluation-reward, while in the case of budgeting the piece lacking is the evaluation-reward system.   The role of accounting systems in organizational controls is examined in Chapter 8.

The Feedback System

Feedback consists of information about operations and their results.   There are two types of feedback: 1) corrective and 2) evaluative.   Corrective feedback is simply information about the performance of the operational system which is designed to help adjust operations in order to improve performance.   Evaluative feedback is information about how well the operational system is doing.   It provides a basis for performance evaluation as well as the administration of rewards.   The role of feedback in control will be examined in greater depth in Chapter 4, together with the role of measurement.

The Evaluation and Reward Subsystem

The evaluation-reward system refers to the mechanisms for performance assessment and the administration of rewards. Rewards are outcomes of behavior which are desirable to a person. Although rewards can either be extrinsic or intrinsic, those used in the evaluation-reward system are extrinsic. The role of the evaluation and reward systems in control are examined in Chapters 5 and 6, respectively.

Illustration of Core Control System

To illustrate the framework for core control system, we will examine the application of the model in a manufacturing plant. As seen in Figure 2-3, the plant has five key result areas: production volume, quality, safety, energy utilization, and scrap. All of these key result areas are different in nature. Production volume is something that can be easily quantified. Energy utilization and scrap can also be measured but in a different way. Quality and safety require still a different type of measurement.

The company has established goals for each of these five key result areas, as listed in the column titled "This Year's Goals." The firm also shows last year's actual performance in the next column. In addition, this year's performance is tracked on a monthly basis in the adjacent columns.

Virtually any company or any unit of a company can use a format similar to that shown in Figure 2-3 to apply the control model to its operations. This approach can be useful for the company as a whole, a division, a department, or even an individual such as a salesperson. Indeed, I observed an example of the application of this framework on a visit to China in 1983 in a chemical plant located in the city of Shanghai. The plant manager was using a blackboard to list the key result areas, current performance goals, prior year's actual performance, and historical best performance, as well as to track the actual performance of the plant to date. Whenever an employee walked past the blackboard, he or she got a quick glimpse at how the plant was performing to date.

Different Configurations of Core Control Systems Elements

Although the four basic elements of the core control systems must be present for the system to function fully, it is possible to find in actual organizational settings different configurations of one or more of the system's elements. For example, it is possible to observe a "control system" that consists merely of a planning system with little else. In such situations measurements may be available only at year end and thus are not available for periodic assessment of performance on a real time basis. On the contrary, performance measurement systems may be found in situations without any formal system for planning and goal-setting. In these situations, it is not possible to evaluate actual performance in relation to plans or budgets.

Figure 2-3: Control Model's Application in Manufacturing Plan

Key Result Areas	This Year's Goals	Last Year's Actual	This Year's Performance											
			Jan.	Feb.	Mar.	Apr.	May	June	July	Aug.	Sep.	Oct.	Nov.	Dec.
1. Production Volume														
2. Quality														
3. Safety														
4. Energy Utilization														
5. Scrap														

A major consequence of the existence of different configurations of core control systems elements is that each observed control system may be expected to produce different degrees of control. Accordingly, it is useful to conceive of "control" as a variable, where the amount of control is a function of the configuration of control system elements.

For conceptual purposes, it may be useful to think of control as achieving different degrees or "control levels," according to the number of control system elements which comprise the system, as represented in Figure 2-4. By definition, if none of the four elements of the core control system are present we shall define this condition as first degree control. In this condition, there are merely operations (decision and actions) which produce results. Control occurs as a by-product of personnel supervision. This type of condition is not uncommon, and, indeed, is characteristic of entrepreneurships and relatively small businesses. Second degree control consists of operations plus any) one additional element: planning, measurement, or evaluation-reward. For example, an organization may have a measurement system without formal planning or even without any system for performance assessment and the administration of rewards. Similarly, different combinations and configurations of control system elements may exist as illustrated in Figure 2-4. This conceptualization may be used both in understanding the effects and defects of control systems as well as a guide to their evaluation design.

Organizational Structure as a Component of Control

The second component of the overall control system shown previously in Figure 2-1 is organizational structure. As Otley and Berry state: "Indeed, organization can itself be view to co-operate in order to achieve purposes which require their joint actions."[15] Similarly, Etzioni states that "organizations theorists have argued that organization structure is developed as a response to the problem of control.[16]

Specifically, structure functions as a control mechanism both by specifying the behaviors expected from people in the performance of their roles, as well as by specifying the authority and reporting relationship of the entire set of roles which comprise the organizational structure, per se. Thus, several structural dimensions contribute to the process of control including the degree of centralization or decentralization, functional specialization, degree of vertical or horizontal integration, and the "span of control" (number of direct reports).

In contrast with the core control system, organization structure is relatively static. It represents a strategic responses to the requirements of markets, technology, and the environment.[17] The role of organization structure in control of is described in Chapter 7.

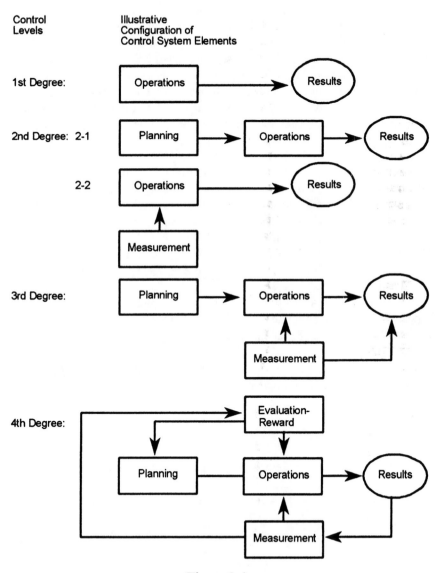

Figure 2-4
Levels of Control Achieved by
Different Configurations of System Elements

Organizational Culture as a Component of Control

The term "culture" is subject to many different definitions and denotations. Kroeber and Kluckholm devoted an entire book to a study of the history, definitions, and properties of the nature of culture.[18] Elsewhere Kluckholm stated that: "Culture consists in patterned ways of thinking, feeling and reacting, acquired and transmitted mainly by symbols, constituting the distinctive achievement of human groups, including their embodiments in artifacts; the essential core of culture consists of traditional (i.e. historically derived and selected) ideas and especially their attached values."[19] In an organizational context, Ouchi refers to culture as the broader values and normative patterns which guide worker behavior, practices and policies.[20] In this chapter, we shall refer to organization culture as the set of values, beliefs, and social norms which tend to be shared by its members and, in turn, tend to influence their thoughts and actions.

Although culture is shown as the third circle in Figure 2-1, it is, in fact, the starting point for the design of an organizational control system. In spite of the fact that it changes slowly and typically with great difficulty, organizational culture is a variable[21]. It is subject to design, and can be the product of management decision. For example, in the early 1980s the Board of Directors of U.S. based RCA Corp. decided to replace that company's president, Edgar H. Griffiths, with Thornton F. Bradshaw. Accordingly to an analysis presented in Business Week, Bradshaw was chosen explicitly to change RCAs culture. His task is to change the value system in the company from on that stresses short-term projects and planning to long range goals. Business Week quoted an unidentified "source close to the Board," as stating that under Griffiths: "Long-range planning meant, `What are we going to do after lunch'" In addition, Bradshaw "...must redirect the culture of the company from one based on intense politicking to one that rewards performance."[22] The role of organizational culture in control is examined in greater depth in Chapter 7.

USES OF THE CONTROL SYSTEMS MODEL

The control systems model presented above has two major, related uses:

1. It can be used to describe and understand the structure of the control systems in actual operating organizations, and
2. It can be used to evaluate the functioning and effectiveness of such systems.

Describing Control Systems Structure

If we wish to get a picture of the structure of an organization, one way is to view an "organization chart," which specifies the roles of people and their nominal relationships. Admittedly, the organization chart is imperfect, because the actual organizational structure is typically far more complex than can be reduced to such a chart. Nevertheless, it does provide a first-approximation for describing an organization.

If we wish to get a picture of the structure of an organization's control system, we need something comparable to an organization chart, which will specify the elements of the control system and their interrelationships. For this purpose, we can develop schematics such as those shown previously in Figure 2-1 to 2-3. We shall term these "Control Systems Charts" because they diagram different aspects of an organization's control systems.

Evaluating the System

Another related use of the model presented above is in evaluating the functioning and effectiveness of the system in an organization. Using control systems charts we can determine whether:

1. All three of the major elements of a control system have been sufficiently developed (culture, structure, and the core control system);
2. All three of the major elements articulate with one another;
3. All the components of the core control system (planning, measurement, etc.) have been developed sufficiently; and
4. All the components of the core control system articulate with each other.

Items 1 and 3 refer to the development of pieces of the control system, while items 2 and 4 relate to their articulations or parts of an integrated system.

In some cases, not all the required parts of a control system may be in place. In others, all of the pieces may be present but may not articulate as a system with each other.

ILLUSTRATION OF THE MODEL'S APPLICATION

In this section we shall examine the control system of an actual company to illustrate the practical use of the model in describing and evaluating the system. The firm is a medium-sized U.S. real estate company located in a large metropolitan area.

Description of Firm

The firm is a residential real estate company. It provides a full set of services (brokerage, property management, leasing, etc.) to buyers of residential real estate throughout a relatively large metropolitan area in a major U.S. city. The firm's organizational structure is shown in Figure 2-5.

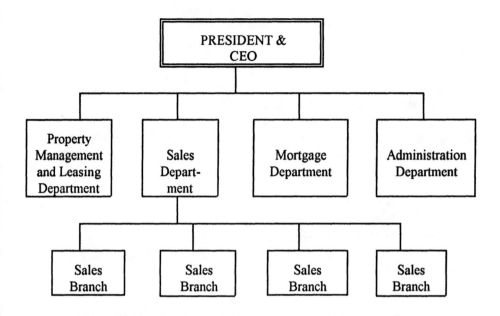

Figure 2-5
Organizational Structure of Metropolitan
Residential Real Estate Firm

At the time of the study, the firm had 12 sales branches located through-out the metropolitan area. Each branch was headed by a branch manager who was supposed to be responsible for branch revenue and costs. Thus technically each branch constituted a profit center. Branches typically had between 10-25 "sales associates" (sales personnel) and 1-2 clerical personnel. The annual volume of residential real estate sold was approximately $300 million.

Firm's Culture, Structure and Budgeting Prior to Study

Residential real estate firms in the U.S. are sales oriented. They tend to be entrepreneurships begun by one or a few people who were initially successful sales-persons themselves and founded their own companies because of available business. Neither the owners or manager in residential real estate firms typically have formal management training or managerial experience in other industries. Thus the culture found in such firms may be characterized as a sales culture. Accordingly, the explicit and implicit value system of the firm emphasizes sales: "listing" of properties to be sold and sales of properties.[23] The culture also states that sales is a "numbers game." If you make so many calls, house showings, etc. you will get listings and sales, and, in turn, earn income.

Branch managers tend almost exclusively to be former salespersons who have been promoted. Few real estate firms have formal training programs for recently promoted managers. They are expected to learn by doing the job.

Since the firms are entrepreneurial in style, there are not typically job descriptions for branch manager, or if role descriptions exist, they tend to be vague. Accordingly, the branch manager tends to define his/her own job and, not surprisingly, the notion of the jobs often emphasize the sale component or things which support sales, rather than such administrative matters as budgeting, planning, cost control, etc.

Branch managers receive a base compensation of "X" thousand dollars per month. In addition, they receive an "override" of 1% of "Company Dollars," (Gross Commissions income received by the firm less Salesperson's share).

The Control Problem

The basic problem with respect to control in this firm is that branch managers paid little or no attention to the budget or variances. They virtually ignored the income statement. Stated simply, branch managers ignored variances, large or small. Many, if not all, hardly looked at the budget or income statement.

The theoretical as well as practical managerial question underlying this behavior may be stated quite simply: Why did the branch managers ignore the firm's income statement and budget variances? To answer this question we shall draw upon the meta-framework of control to examine the elements of culture, organizational structure, and core control system. Taken together, an analysis of these elements explains the very rational behavior of branch managers in ignoring income statements and budgets.

Culture and Budget Control

The firm's culture unintentionally mitigated against branch managers paying attention to budgets, income statements, and, indeed, even profits; the culture emphasized SALES in all capital letters. The explicit value system as well as the informal socialization system all held the successful salesperson in high regard. This carried over to successful branch managers; they were successful if they could attract, motivate, and retain "top sales people."

Organizational Structure and Budgetary Control

The role of sales managers was a sales oriented role. In addition to the ability to recruit and manage personnel, the sales managers must be knowledgeable about real estate transactions both to train sales associates and to serve as a consultant on complex transactions. Knowledge of accounting and budgetary controls skills are not explicitly viewed as part of the role and, if present, are not highly valued.

The Core Control System and Budgetary Control

The firm's core control system was not explicitly designed as such. There is a plan (budget), a measurement system (the accounting system), feedback (budget reports and income statements), and an evaluation-reward system (performance appraisal and compensation systems). However, these components or subsystems have not been designed either: 1) explicitly to lead to emphasis on profits and attention to variances from profit budgets, or 2) to articulate with one another in an integrated fashion. The former problem concerns the purposes of the system, while the latter concerns the system's architecture or structure.

In the language of the firm's culture, the branch managers do not perceive "ownership of the budget." It is not their budget, but top management's budget. There is also a problem with the accounting system as it relates to providing information for real time decisions and control. In a sales culture such as this, the art of completing a contract of sale is the major point of psychological closure for a salesperson and a branch manager. From both a legal and accounting point of view, however, the transaction is not completed (final) until the deal "closes" (that is, all the conditions of the transactions have been satisfied and money and deeds to property are exchanged). The "closing" may occur 30-60-90 days or more after the deal has been reached, and by this time salespersons and branch managers are absorbed by other potential transactions. To deal with the uncertainty in realization of income, the firm's accounting system either operates on a cash basis under which income is realized and commissions paid when escrow closes, or on an accrual basis with an "allowance for cancellations" which is similar but not identical to an allowance for uncollectables.

Thus there is a conflict between the psychological mind set of branch managers with respect to income "earned" and the accounting definition of income earned as well as the financial reporting of such income. This difference has led the managers to reject and ridicule accountants and accounting systems while still being forced to accept their dictates. Consequently, the numbers generated by the accounting system as reported in Company income statements are viewed as irrelevant to managers for action taking purposes. The numbers affect the timing of the managers compensation, but are not seen as useful.

In addition, the most relevant numbers concern sales revenues not net profit, because the compensation system provides for an override (bonus) based upon sales not branch profits. This is congruent with the sales-oriented culture of the firm, rather than economic theory. It is an instance of what Kerr has referred to as "the folly of rewarding A, while hoping for B."[24]

Discussion of the System

The operation of the control system at this U.S. real estate company helps to illustrate the usefulness of the model presented above. First, the firm's control system cannot be viewed merely as a set of control techniques such as budget or accounting measurements and reports; these control mechanisms did not motivate and control the behavior of the firm's managers.

The real control system must be viewed as the combination of the firm's culture, structure, budgetary planning, and accounting measurement system, as summarized in Figure 2-6. A detailed description of the specific aspects of the firm's control system is shown in Figure 2-7.

Figure 2-6
Metropolitan Residential Real Estate Firm
Diagrammatic Description of Control System

Elements of Control	**Metropolitan Residential Real Estate Firm**
1.0 Organizational Culture	1.1 Values:

        A.   Emphasis on "sales": listings & sales of properties.

        B.   Real estate is a "numbers game."

        C.   Branch managers are former sales persons.

        D.   Learning by on-the-job doing.

        E.   The successful sales person is held in high esteem.

        F.   Managers are successful if they attract, motivate, and retain "top sales people."

2.0 Organizational Structure

2.1 There are no job descriptions.

2.2 The branch manager's role emphasizes sales not administration.

3.0 Core Control System

3.1 The firm's core control system was not designed as such.

3.2 There is a formal budget.

3.3 Accounting for transactions differs from psychological closure.

3.4 The accounting system measures results.

3.5 Results and variances are reported.

3.6 The compensation system rewards sales, not meeting budget.

Figure 2-7
Metropolitan Residential Real Estate Firm Summary of Control System

Using the framework developed in this chapter, these two charts help to make the firm's control system explicit. We can see that although the firm's president states that its objective is to control <u>profitability</u>, the system actually focuses upon sales. Thus it is quite natural for the branch managers to pay little or no attention to the budget or variances.

If the firm wishes to change the behavior of its managers, it must revise its control system. The firm's culture ought to be revised to focus upon profits rather than sales; the organizational structure and managerial role needs to be revised, and, also, the core control system. Chapter 9 shall deal with the process of making such changes in the design of control systems.

CONCLUSION

This chapter has presented a framework for describing and analyzing an organization's control system. The framework consists of three major parts: 1) A core control system, 2) Organizational structure, and 3) Organizational culture. The core control system consists, in turn, of five basic organizational processes or components: Planning, operations, measurement, feedback, and evaluation-reward. Each of these components of the core control system are organizational systems per se.

The role of each of these major parts of a control system (the core control system, structure, and culture) will be examined in the remaining chapters. First, we shall examine the components of the core control system (chapters three through six). Then we shall examine the role of structure and culture in organizational control (chapter seven).

This chapter also illustrates the practical use of this framework into the context of an actual organization: It described the control problems of a residential real estate firm, and illustrated how we can use the control systems framework to understand why the organization's control system is not effective in motivating it desired results.

ENDNOTES

9. This chapter draws upon Eric G. Flamholtz, "Accounting, Budgeting, and Control Systems in
    Their Organizational Context: Theoretical and Empirical Perspectives, Accounting,
    Organizations and Society, Vol. 8, Number 2/3, 1983, pp. 153-169.
10. The model used in this chapter is adopted from E.G. Flamholtz, T.K. Das, and A.S. Tsui,
    "Toward and Integrative Framework of Organizational Control," Accounting, Organizations and
    Society, Vol. 10, No. 1, 1985, pp. 35-50, which, in turn, was an elaboration and extension of a
    previous model by E.G. Flamholtz, "Organizational Control Systems as a Managerial Tool,"
    California Management Review, Vol. 22, No. 2, Winter 1979, pp. 50-59.
11. Hofstede, G., "The Poverty of Management Control Philosophy," Academy of Management
    Review, July 1978, pp. 450-461.
    Otley, D.T. and Berry, A.J., "Control, Organizations and Accounting," Accounting,
    Organizations and Society, Vol. 5, No. 2, pp. 231-244.
    Weiner, N., Cybernetics, Cambridge, MA: M.I.T. Press, 1948.
12. The problem of reification need not hinder us if we view the "organization" as a proprietorship,
    dominant coalition, or institution comprised of individuals and groups.
13. Hall, F.S., "Organizational Goals: The Status of Theory and Research", in J.L. Livingstone
    (Ed.), Managerial Accounting: The Behavioral Foundations, Columbus, Ohio: Grid Publishing
    Company, 1975, pp.1-32.
14. Cammann, C., "Effects of the Use of Control Systems," Accounting, Organizations and Society,
    Vol. 1, No. 4, 1976, pp. 301-314.
    Flamholtz, E.G., "Toward A Psycho-Technical Systems Paradigm of Organizational
    Measurement," Decision Sciences, January 1979, pp. 71-84.
    Prakash, P. and Rappaport, A., "Information Inductance and Its Significance for Accounting,"
    Accounting, Organizations and Society, 1977, pp. 29-38.
    Williams, J.J. and C.R. Hinings, " A Note on Matching Control System Implications with
    Organizational Characteristics: ZBB and MBO Revisited", Accounting, Organizations and
    Society, 1988, pp. 191-200.
15. Otley, D.T. and Berry, A.J., "Control, Organizations and Accounting," Accounting,
    Organizations and Society, Vol. 5, No. 2, pp. 231-244.
16. Blau, P.N. and Scott, W., Formal Organizations, San Francisco: Chandler, 1962.
    Etzioni, A., A Comparative Analysis of Complex Organizations, Glencoe, IL: Free Press, 1961.
    Perrow, C., "The Bureaucratic Paradox, The Efficient Organization Centralizes in Order to
    Decentralize," Organization Dynamics, 1977, pp. 3-14.
    Poole, M.S. and A.H. Van De Ven, "Using Paradox to Build Management and Organization
    Theories", Academy of Management Review, 1989, 14: 562-578.
17. Child, J., "Organizational Growth," in S. Kerr (Ed.), Organizational Behavior, Columbus, Ohio:
    Grid Publishing Company, Inc., 1979, Chapter 16, pp. 379-399.
    Yasai-Ardekani, Masoud, "Effects of Environmental Scarcity and Munificence on the
    Relationship of Context to Organizational Structure", Academy of Management Journal, 1989,
    32: 131-156.
    Keats, Barbara W and Michael A Hitt, "Causal Model of Linkages Among Environmental
    Dimensions and Macro Organizational Characteristics," Academy of Management Journal,
    1988, 31: 570-598.
    Miller, Danny, Cornelia Droge, and Jean-Marie Toulouse, "Strategic Process and Content as
    Mediators Between Organizational Context and Structure", Academy of Management Journal,
    1988, 544-569.
18. Kroeber, A.L. and Kluckhohn, C., Culture: A critical Review of Concepts and Definitions, New
    York: Vintage Books, 1952.
19. Kluckhohn, C., "The Study of Culture," in D. Lerner and H.D. Laswell (Eds.), the Policy
    Sciences, Stanford, CA: Stanford University Press, 1951, pp. 86-101.

ENDNOTES

9. This chapter draws upon Eric G. Flamholtz, "Accounting, Budgeting, and Control Systems in Their Organizational Context: Theoretical and Empirical Perspectives, <u>Accounting, Organizations and Society</u>, Vol. 8, Number 2/3, 1983, pp. 153-169.

10. The model used in this chapter is adopted from E.G. Flamholtz, T.K. Das, and A.S. Tsui, "Toward and Integrative Framework of Organizational Control," <u>Accounting, Organizations and Society</u>, Vol. 10, No. 1, 1985, pp. 35-50, which, in turn, was an elaboration and extension of a previous model by E.G. Flamholtz, "Organizational Control Systems as a Managerial Tool," <u>California Management Review</u>, Vol. 22, No. 2, Winter 1979, pp. 50-59.

11. Hofstede, G., "The Poverty of Management Control Philosophy," <u>Academy of Management Review</u>, July 1978, pp. 450-461.
    Otley, D.T. and Berry, A.J., "Control, Organizations and Accounting," <u>Accounting, Organizations and Society</u>, Vol. 5, No. 2, pp. 231-244.
    Weiner, N., <u>Cybernetics</u>, Cambridge, MA: M.I.T. Press, 1948.

12. The problem of reification need not hinder us if we view the "organization" as a proprietorship, dominant coalition, or institution comprised of individuals and groups.

13. Hall, F.S., "Organizational Goals: The Status of Theory and Research", in J.L. Livingstone (Ed.), <u>Managerial Accounting: The Behavioral Foundations</u>, Columbus, Ohio: Grid Publishing Company, 1975, pp.1-32.

14. Cammann, C., "Effects of the Use of Control Systems," <u>Accounting, Organizations and Society</u>, Vol. 1, No. 4, 1976, pp. 301-314.
    Flamholtz, E.G., "Toward A Psycho-Technical Systems Paradigm of Organizational Measurement," <u>Decision Sciences</u>, January 1979, pp. 71-84.
    Prakash, P. and Rappaport, A., "Information Inductance and Its Significance for Accounting," <u>Accounting, Organizations and Society</u>, 1977, pp. 29-38.
    Williams, J.J. and C.R. Hinings, " A Note on Matching Control System Implications with Organizational Characteristics: ZBB and MBO Revisited", <u>Accounting, Organizations and Society</u>, 1988, pp. 191-200.

15. Otley, D.T. and Berry, A.J., "Control, Organizations and Accounting," <u>Accounting, Organizations and Society</u>, Vol. 5, No. 2, pp. 231-244.

16. Blau, P.N. and Scott, W., <u>Formal Organizations</u>, San Francisco: Chandler, 1962.
    Etzioni, A., <u>A Comparative Analysis of Complex Organizations</u>, Glencoe, IL: Free Press, 1961.
    Perrow, C., "The Bureaucratic Paradox, The Efficient Organization Centralizes in Order to Decentralize," <u>Organization Dynamics</u>, 1977, pp. 3-14.
    Poole, M.S. and A.H. Van De Ven, "Using Paradox to Build Management and Organization Theories", Academy of Management Review, 1989, 14: 562-578.

17. Child, J., "Organizational Growth," in S. Kerr (Ed.), <u>Organizational Behavior</u>, Columbus, Ohio: Grid Publishing Company, Inc., 1979, Chapter 16, pp. 379-399.
    Yasai-Ardekani, Masoud, "Effects of Environmental Scarcity and Munificence on the Relationship of Context to Organizational Structure", <u>Academy of Management Journal</u>, 1989, 32: 131-156.
    Keats, Barbara W and Michael A Hitt, "Causal Model of Linkages Among Environmental Dimensions and Macro Organizational Characteristics," <u>Academy of Management Journal</u>, 1988, 31: 570-598.
    Miller, Danny, Cornelia Droge, and Jean-Marie Toulouse, "Strategic Process and Content as Mediators Between Organizational Context and Structure", <u>Academy of Management Journal</u>, 1988, 544-569.

18. Kroeber, A.L. and Kluckhohn, C., <u>Culture: A critical Review of Concepts and Definitions</u>, New York: Vintage Books, 1952.

19. Kluckhohn, C., "The Study of Culture," in D. Lerner and H.D. Laswell (Eds.), <u>the Policy Sciences</u>, Stanford, CA: Stanford University Press, 1951, pp. 86-101.

20. Ouchi, W., "A Conceptual Framework for the Design of Organizational Control Mechanisms," Management Science, 1979, 25, pp. 833-847.

21. The following research looks at the process of changing organization culture:
Nahavandi, A. and A.R. Malekzadeh, " Acculturation in Mergers and Acquisitions", 1988, Academy of Management Review, 13: 79-90.
Weiner, Y., "Forms of Value Systems: a Focus on Organizational Effectiveness and Cultural Change and Maintenance", Academy of Management Review, 13: 534-545
Eisenhardt, K.M. and C.B. Schoonhoven,"Organizational Growth: Linking Founding Team, Strategy, Environment, and Growth Among U.S. Semiconductor Ventures, 1978-1988", Administrative Science Quarterly, 35: 504-525.
The relationship between a culture and its subcultures is explored in S.A. Sackman's "Culture and Subcultures: An Analysis of Organizational Knowledge", Administrative Science Quarterly, 37: 140-161.
Measuring and comparing organization cultures is explored in G. Hofstede et al.'s "Measuring Organizational Cultures: A Qualitative and Quantitative Study Across Twenty Cases", Administrative Science Quarterly, 35: 286-305.

22. Business Week Staff, "Why Griffiths is Out as RCA Chairman," Business Week, February 9, 1981, pp. 72-73.

23. A "listing" is a contract between the principal (property owner) and agent (broker for the latter) to have exclusive rights to sell property.

24. Kerr, S., "On The Folly of Rewarding A, While Hoping For B," Academy of Management Journal, December 1975, pp. 769-783.

REFERENCES

Blau, P.N. and Scott, W., Formal Organizations, San Francisco: Chandler, 1962.

Business Week Staff, "Why Griffiths is Out as RCA Chairman, Business Week, February 9, 1981, pp. 72-73.

Child, J., "Organizational Growth," in S. Kerr (Ed.), Organizational Behavior, Columbus, Ohio: Grid Publishing Co., Inc., 1979, Chapter 16, pp. 379-399.

Cammann, C., "Effects of the Use of Control Systems," Accounting, Organizations and Society, 1, 4, 1976, pp. 301-314.

Egelhoff, W.G., Organizing the Multinational Enterprise: An Information Processing Perspective, Cambridge, MA: Ballinger, 1988.

Eisenhardt, K.M., "Control: Organizational and Economic Approaches," Management Science, Vol. 41, 1985, pp. 134-149.

Eisenhardt, K.M. and C.B. Schoonhoven, "Organizational Growth: Linking Founding Team, Strategy, Environment, and Growth Among U.S. Semiconductor Ventures, 1978-1988", Administrative Science Quarterly, 1990, 35:504-525.

Etzioni, A., A Comparative Analysis of Complex Organizations, Glencoe, IL: Free Press, 1961.

Flamholtz, E.G.,"Accounting, Budgeting, and Control Systems in Their Organizational Context: Theoretical and Empirical Perspectives", Accounting, Organizations and Society

Flamholtz, E.G., "Organizational Control Systems as a Managerial Tool," California Management Review, Vol. 22, No. 2, Winter 1979, pp. 50-59.

Flamholtz, E.G., "Toward A Psycho-Technical Systems Paradigm of Organizational Measurement," Decision Sciences, January 1979, pp. 71-84.

Flamholtz, E.G., Das, T.K. and Tsui, A., "Towards an Integrative Theory of Organizational Control," Accounting, Organizations and Society, Vol. 10, No. 1, 1985, pp. 35-50.

Govindarajan, V. and Gupta, A.K., "Linking Control Systems to Business Unit Strategy: Impact on Performance," Accounting, Organizations and Society, Vol. 10, No. 1, 1985, pp. 51-66.

Gupta, A.K. and Govindarajan, V., "Knowledge Flows and the Structure of Control Within Multinational Organizations," The Academy of Management Review, Vol. 10, No. 4, October 1991, pp. 768-792.

Hall, F.S., "Organizational Goals: The Status of Theory and Research," in J.L. Livingstone (Ed.), Managerial Accounting: The Behavioral Foundations, Columbus, Ohio: Grid Publishing Co, 1975, pp. 1-32.

Hofstede, G., "The Poverty of Management Control Philosophy," Academy of Management Review, July 1978, pp. 450-461.

Hofstede, G. B. Neuijen, D.D. Ohayv, and G. Sanders, "Measuring Organizational Cultures: A Qualitative and Quanitative Study across Twenty Cases", Administrative Science Quarterly, 1990, 35:286-305.

Keats, Barbara W. and Michael A. Hitt, "Causal Model of Linkages Among the Environmental Dimensions and Macro Organizational Characteristics," Academy of Management Journal, 1988,31: 570-598.

Kerr, S., "On The Folly of Rewarding A, While Hoping For B," Academy of Management Journal, December 1975, pp. 769-783.

Kluckhohn, C., "The Study of Culture," in D. Lerner and H.D. Laswell (Eds.), The Policy Sciences, Stanford, CA: Stanford University Press, 1951, pp. 86-101.

Kroeber, A.L. and Kluckhohn, C., Culture: A Critical Review of Concepts and Definitions, New York: Vintage Books, 1952.

Martinez, J.I. and Jarillo, J.C., "The Evolution of Research on Coordination Mechanisms in Multinational Corporations," Journal of International Business Studies, 1989.

Miller, Danny, Cornelia Droge, and Jean-Marie Toulouse, "Strategic Process and Content as Mediators Between Organizational Context and Structure", Academy of Management Journal, 1988,31:544-569.

Nahavandi, A. and A.R. Malekzadeh, "Acculturation in Mergers and Acquisitions", 1988, Academy of Management Review, 13: 79-90.

Otley, D.T. and Berry, A.J., "Control, Organizations and Accounting," Accounting, Organizations and Society, 5, 2, pp. 231-244.

Ouchi, W., "A Conceptual Framework for the Design of Organizational Control Mechanisms," Management Science, 1979, 25, pp. 833-847.

Perrow, C., "The Bureaucratic Paradox, The Efficient Organization Centralizes in Order to Decentralize," Organization Dynamics, 1977, pp. 3-14.

Poole, M.S. and A.H. Van De Ven, "Using Paradox to Build Management and Organization Theories", Academy of Management Review, 1989, 14:562-568.

Prakash, P. and Rappaport, A., "Information Inductance and Its Significance for Accounting," Accounting, Organizations and Society, 1977, pp. 29-38.

Sackman, S.A., "Culture and Subcultures: An Analysis of Organizational Knowledge", Administrative Science Quarterly, 1992, 37: 140-161.

Weiner, N., Cybernetics, Cambridge, MA: M.I.T. Press, 1948.

Weiner, Y., "Forms of Value Systems: A Focus on Organizational Effectiveness and Cultural Change and Maintenance", Academy of Management Review, 13: 534-545.

Williams, J.J. and C.R. Hinings, "A Note on Matching Control System Implications and Organizational Characteristics: ZBB and MBO Revisited:, Accounting, Organizations and Society, 1988, pp 191-200.

Yasai-Ardekani, Masoud, "Effects of Environmental Scarcity and Muniference on the Relationship of Context to Organizational Structure," Academy of Management Journal, 1989,32:131-156.

3

THE ROLE OF PLANNING
IN CONTROL

In its broadest sense, "planning" is the process of deciding about the objectives of an organization and the ways to attain those objectives. It involves analyzing an organization's environment, assessing potential opportunities, formulating general objectives and specific goals, as well as developing action plans to attain them.

Although many organizations develop plans, not all organizations which have them are successful in their implementation. In many organizations, once plans are made, they tend to gather dust and are not meaningful as a management tool. This problem typically occurs because the planning system in an enterprise is seen as something independent from the organization's control system. This suggests that we need to understand the relationship between planning and control as a vehicle to better implement an organization's plans.

There is also another reason for examining the relationship between planning and control, and that is because planning plays a critical role in the process of organizational control itself. The planning system is itself an integral part of an overall control system. In fact, it is the starting point for the entire control process.

This chapter, therefore, suggests the need to examine the symbiotic relationship between planning and control. First we shall examine the nature of planning per se, as well as the components of the planning process. Then we will examine the relationship between planning and control, and the role that planning plays as part of a control system. An implicit assumption here is that planning is perhaps better understood as a component of an overall control system, rather than as a stand alone process per se.

ACTION DEFINITION OF PLANNING

An "action definition" (or operational definition) tells us not only what something is, but how to do it. Defined in action-oriented terms, planning is the process of deciding about the:

1. "mission" of the organization,
2. "key result areas" for planning,
3. "objectives" and "goals" in each area, and

4. "action plans" to attain them.

This definition treats planning as a set of four related steps. First, the organization's mission must be defined. Next, the key result areas necessary to accomplish the mission are developed. Then objectives and goals are established for each key result area. Finally, action plans are developed for achieving each goal.

These four components of the planning system are shown schematically in Figure 3-1.

COMPONENTS OF THE PLANNING SYSTEM

This section describes and illustrates the four components of a planning system: mission, key result areas, objectives and goals, and action plans. Each component is examined, in turn, below.

Mission

A mission is a broad statement of what an organization or subunit wants to achieve during the planning period. It provides an overall sense of directions to decisions and actions. Selected examples are presented below.

An example of a mission statement for a corporation that is an industrial abrasive distributor is:

> "To develop into the leading full service distributor of industrial abrasives in the western United States by 1998."

This is a broad statement of what Industrial Abrasives, Inc. wants to achieve by the end of a five year planning period.

Another example of a mission statement for a medium-sized residential real estate firm is:

> "To develop into a full service residential real estate company, providing services throughout the northern part of the state. In order to become a full service residential real estate firm, we must add to the present service capabilities in: guaranteed sales, condo-conversion, tract sales, investment counseling, and primary mortgages."

This is a broad statement of what Industrial Abrasives, Inc. wants to achieve by the end of a five year planning period.

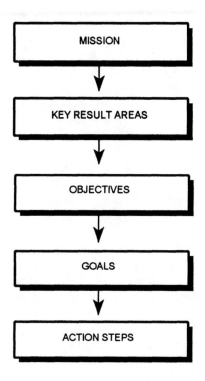

1. Mission   -   Broad statement of what the organization wants to achieve during the planning period.

2. Key Result Areas   -   These are the performance areas that are critical to achieving the organization's mission.

3. Objectives   -   These are what the organization wants to achieve in the long run in each key result area.

4. Goals   -   These are specific things that the organization seeks to attain by a specified time.

5. Action Plans   -   These are activities which must be performed to achieve a specific goal.

Figure 3-1
Components of the Planning System

Another example of a mission statement for a medium-sized residential real estate firm is:

> "To develop into a full service residential real estate company, providing services throughout the northern part of the state. In order to become a full service residential real estate firm, we must add to the present service capabilities in: guaranteed sales, condo-conversion, tract sales, investment counseling, and primary mortgages."

The mission of an airline company, such as SAS or TWA, might be:

> "To make the transition from an airline company to a diversified travel company."

In fact, this was, during the 1980's, the actual mission of United Airlines (UAL), which, briefly changed its name to Allegis to reflect this change before it reversed its strategic direction. As part of its strategic plan, UAL had acquired hotels (The Westin and Hilton International chains), a car rental company (Hertz), and had established its own travel company.

Another type of mission is one developed by a large national certified public accounting (CPA) firm:

> "Our mission is to develop a profitable, professional international accounting firm with a dynamic environment that will retain and motivate outstanding people who will provide high quality services to business, government, and not-for-profit clients."

Missions can be developed not only for an organization as a whole, but for specific subunits as well. For example, the mission statement for the personnel department of a bank with assets in excess of $1 billion is:

> "The mission of the personnel department is to assist management with the attainment of its goals and objectives by:
> 1) developing the capability to identify and meet the human resource needs of the bank, and
> 2) developing the capability to help our people resource utilize their skills to the optimum.

In brief, the mission statement is the starting point of the planning process.

Key Result Areas

Key result areas are areas of an organization's operation where performance has a critical impact upon the achievement of the overall mission. If performance in a key result area is unsatisfactory, it will inhibit the organization from achieving its mission.

The specific key result areas vary from organization to organization and each firm must identify those which are relevant to its mission. In the industrial abrasives firm cited above, there were five key result areas:

1. profitability,
2. financial planning,
3. management and organizational development,
4. physical plan and equipment, and
5. marketing capabilities.

In the residential real estate firm, key results were classified into two groups: 1) financial results, and 2) non-financial results. In the financial result area, there were two major dimensions: 1) company profitability, and 2) profit contribution by departments of the firm. In the non-financial area, there were five key result dimensions:

1. company integration,
2. services offered,
3. personnel development,
4. administration of the firm, and
5. research.

The specific key result areas for a department, division, or other subunit of a firm will differ from those of the overall entity. For example, the key result areas for the personnel department of a bank were:

1. recruitment and selection of staff,
2. compensation and benefits administration,
3. availability of personnel data to meet management information needs,
4. turnover control,
5. advisor on personnel matters to management and employees,
6. knowledge of EEO, ERISA, OSHA regulations, etc.,
7. communication,
8. training, and
9. personnel research.

In brief, key result areas are an outgrowth of the mission, and vary from organization to organization.

Objectives and Goals

Objectives are things which an organization or subunit wants to achieve in the long run in each key result area. An objective is a relatively general statement of what is to be achieved in an area, rather than a precise goal. Goals are specific things that the organization wants to attain by a specified time. [25]

For example, an objective for a medium-sized manufacturer of electronic components may be "to increase our annual sales volume," while a specific goal would be: "Increase sales volume from current level of $15 million in 19X5 to $18 million in 19X6." Similarly, an objective in the area of facilities and equipment may be "to increase our capability for inventory storage," while a specific goal would be "to relocate our Midwest branch by 19X6 to a new site capable of handling 150% greater inventory than existing facilities."

In the area of profit, an objective may be "to earn a satisfactory return on investment." A specific goal is: "To earn a minimum of 18% ROI before taxes in each operating division.

In brief, goals are specific things to be accomplished in order to achieve broader objectives.[26] Both objectives and goals are necessary. Objectives are broader and somewhat more vague, but they <u>should</u> <u>not</u> change very frequently during a planning period. Goals are specific but are subject to frequent change.[27] For example, the objective of a marketing department for a large, Fortune 500 manufacturer of electronic equipment is to develop marketing programs for new products. A goals for 19X5 is "to plan a campaign to introduce electronic toys into the market for the winter season."

Action Plans

Action plans specify activities or steps which must be performed to achieve a goal. Although action plans are not necessary for all goals, these are useful for achieving relatively complex projects or tasks.

THE RELATIONSHIP BETWEEN PLANNING AND CONTROL

Although it is not generally perceived, there is essentially a symbiotic relationship between planning and control, Ultimately, to be effective, planning requires control, and vise versa.

Without a control process, planning is either less useful than it can be or completely meaningless. Many corporate plans are developed and then placed in drawers or on a shelf to gather dust. Little or no attention is paid to them, and they have no impact on operations.

To be effective in motivating behavior, plans must be linked to the other components of a core control system: measurement, feedback, evaluation, and rewards. If plans are made with no measurement of progress, no feedback, no link to the performance evaluation process, and no link to rewards, they are not likely to actually motivate people to pursue the planned objectives and goals.

Just as planning is not likely to be effective without being linked to its other components of the core control system, the core control system as a whole is not likely to function well without these key planning components. The control process begins with the planning process. The plan specifies the direction of what the organization wants to achieve. It establishes a mission, key result areas, objectives, and goals. Without these things, control is direction less.

There is, accordingly, a symbiotic or mutually dependent relationship between planning and control. One without the other is, in theory almost unthinkable, but is often observed in practice. This helps to explain why plans so often fail to be implemented as well as why control systems are often ineffective.

The discussion above suggests that the optimal way of thinking about planning is that it is an integral component of an organization's core control system. Since planning is essential for control and since it does not function effectively in isolation, we must treat it as a component of control rather than a stand alone system.

STEPS IN THE PLANNING PROCESS

The components of an organization's planning system were described above. This section presents the steps in the process of developing an organization's plan.

The specific steps in developing a plan are summarized in a flow diagram shown in Figure 3-2. It shows that the development of a formal plan is a seven-step process: beginning from the analysis and definition of a firm's business.

ILLUSTRATION OF DEVELOPMENT OF A PLAN

To illustrate the process and output of an organizational plan, we shall examine the planning process of a service company. The firm is the medium-sized residential real estate company introduced in Chapter 2. We shall refer to this company as "Metropolitan Realty, Inc."

By examining the step by step process of developing a plan for this company, we can better appreciate the meaning of the components of a plan and the nature of the overall

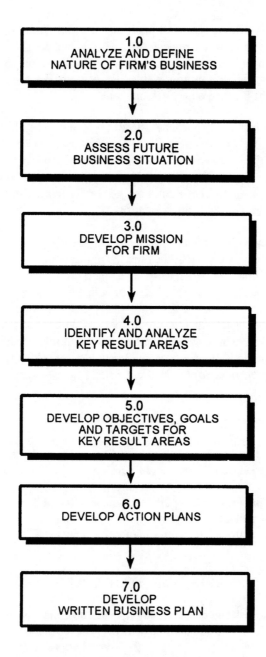

Figure 3-2
Flow Diagram of Steps in the Planning

planning process. This, in turn, will provide a context for illustrating the role of planning in control.

Concept of Business

At present, Metropolitan Realty, Inc. (MRI) is in the process of developing toward a full service real estate business. In the long run, MRI may expand the scope of its business and become a full service real estate firm in commercial as well as residential markets.

As part of the annual planning process MRI identified the alternative concepts of business to guide its operations. The purpose of developing a concept of the business is to provide direction for corporate efforts and to identify or help create a market niche or competitive difference for the company. The alternative concepts of the business are shown in Figure 3-3 and described below.

Specialize in Residential Brokerage

This concept of the business (Concept A) sees MRI specializing in residential real estate brokerage with some minimal level of support from other areas, which operate independently. This is the firm's present strategy. Following this concept MRI would add more brokerage offices and maintain other functional areas of real estate at their present levels.

Full Service Residential Real Estate

Concept (B) would involve becoming a firm capable of serving all of a client's residential real needs. It would involve identifying the full set of services required in residential real estate and building the capability of supplying those services.

Concept B, in contrast to Concept A, views loan, mortgages, relocation, leasing and other areas to be defined as an integral part of MRI and not merely as an adjunct. Under this concept the existence of loan, mortgage, relocation, etc., capability would be an important part of MRI's competitive strength, and the concept of MRI as a full service real estate business would be used in marketing all of the firm's services.

An analysis of MRI's major competitors indicates that most of them are moving toward full service residential real estate firms, with the exception of two major corporations.

Full Service Real Estate Firm

Concept C would extend MRI's services to commercial as well as residential real estate. At present two of MRI's major competitors have developed toward this concept. Although it was felt that in the long run MRI should consider development

Concept A. Specialize in residential real estate brokerage with
minimal <u>support</u> from other areas:

    1. More Offices

    2. Mortgages

    3. Leasing/Property Management

    4. Special Projects

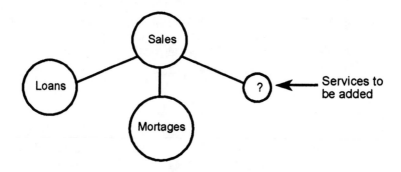

Concept B. Full Service Residential Real Estate Firm

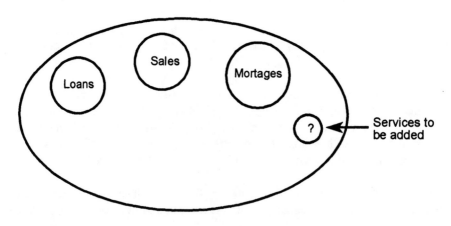

Concept C. Full Service Real Estate Firm

Figure 3-3
Alternative Concepts of Business

toward this type of business, at the present time revenues were not sufficient to allow adoption of this concept.

In order to choose among these concepts at the Annual Review and Planning meeting, a number of questions were analyzed such as those shown in Figure 3-4. It was decided that for the next five years MRI should develop toward the concept of a full service residential real estate firm.

Corporate Mission

Based upon our planning meeting, the mission of MRI is to develop into a full service residential real estate company, providing services throughout the northern part of the state. In order to become a full service residential real estate company MRI must add to its present services capability in the following areas: marketing, guaranteed sales, condo-conversion, tract sales, investment counseling and sales, and primary mortgages.

Objectives

Over the next five years the objectives are to work toward the corporate mission of becoming the leading full service residential real estate firm in the area. In order to do this both financial and non-financial objectives were defined for the period 1991-1995, as follows:

Financial Objectives

Profit - To develop the profitability to a satisfactory level by 1993, through revenue increases and cost control.

Profit Contribution - To develop the company so that there is a balanced profit contribution from each department.

Non-Financial Objectives

Corporate Integration - To achieve the integration of all parts of MRI as a whole so that its functions as a single system rather than as a set of separate entities.

Services - To review new and existing services in order to evaluate each and recommend addition, deletion, or expansion of these services.

Personnel Development - To provide education and training programs for management, sales associates, and administrative salaried personnel.

NO.	PLANNING STEPS	RELATED ISSUES
1.0	Analyze and Define Nature of Firm's Business	1.1 What is the nature of our business? 1.1.1 Services 1.1.2 Markets and customers 1.1.3 Competition 1.2 What is the firm's market niche and competitive advantage? 1.2.1 Do we have a special niche in the market? 1.2.2 What distinguishes us from our competition?
2.0	Assess Future Business Situation	2.1 What will our industry be like in five year? 2.1.1 Trends 2.1.2 Opportunities 2.1.3 Threats
3.0	Develop Mission for Firm	3.1 What do we want to be like or become in five years?
4.0	Identify and Analyze Key Result Areas	4.1 What must the firm do during the next five years to achieve its mission? 4.2 What are the Key Result Areas of the business? 4.3 What are our current strengths and limitations in each Key Result Area?
5.0	Develop Objectives and Goals for Key Result Areas	5.1 What are our objectives in each area? 5.2 What are our goals in each Key Result Area?
6.0	Develop Plans for Implementing Objectives and Goals	6.1 What are our priorities for developing programs in various Key Result Areas? 6.2 Who is responsible for developing programs in each area? 6.3 What steps must be taken to achieve objectives and goals in each result area?
7.0	Develop Written Business Plan	

Figure 3-4
Planning Steps and Related Issues

<u>Administration</u> - To increase administrative efficiency by the improvement of the management reporting system, the adoption of a planning system, and development of a control system, including incentive compensation and performance appraisal.

<u>Research</u> - To develop the capability to do research on important aspects of the business.

Goals

Financial Goals

<u>Profit</u> - To reach profit for 1993-1995 of 10% - minimum, 15% - most likely, and 20% - ideal, of gross revenue, after all costs have been considered.

<u>Revenue</u> - To base revenue on 8% inflation plus 102% "real" growth.

<u>Costs</u> - To establish a standard of costs per employee, both direct and non-direct, with the minimum - $750, most likely - $850, and maximum - $1,000.

Non-Financial Goals

<u>Company Integration</u> - To expand and develop the relocation department so as to increase the number of referrals and integrate the role of the department staff throughout the company.

<u>Services</u> - To evaluate the possibility of new services in the following areas: guaranteed sales, condominium conversion, tract and subdivision sales, primary mortgages, investment and counseling.

<u>Personnel Department</u> - To develop programs in the following major areas: 1) a management development and training program for present members of management and management candidates that will improve the quality of management as well as providing a necessary pool of future managers; 2) an indoctrination program of six full days for all new sales associates joining the firm (presently provided by the Realty Class); 3) on-the-job training for the administrative salaried group to instruct them in their duties and role in the organization.

<u>Administration</u> - To increase efficiency in the following areas: 1) development of the capability to provide accurate and timely accounting reports, and to analyze all current reporting systems to decide if they should be continued, discontinued or expanded; 2)completion of the implementation of the annual planning cycle, including development of an annual written corporate planning guide; 3) development and implementation of a revised incentive compensation system for all managers; 4)development and implementation of a performance appraisal and counseling system

for all managers.

<u>Research</u> - To initiate research projects on the following topics: 1) competitive niche;
2) growth; 3) franchises; 4) question of whether there should be a marketing
department/position.

THE FUNCTION OF PLANNING IN CONTROL

The preceding section has presented portions of a business plan for a company to
illustrate the nature and output of the planning process. As seen in the control systems
model in Chapter 2, planning is the first phase of the control process. It specifies what
the organization seeks to accomplish.

By specifying the organization's direction, a focus for efforts is given. This in itself is
a form of control. However, the more specific statement of key result areas, objectives,
and goals increases the degree and effectiveness of control.

In brief, planning provides the targets for the operational system to achieve. Hence it
represents the beginning of the control process in organizations. A written business
plan, such as the one illustrated for Metropolitan Realty, Inc., helps facilitate the
planning aspect of the control process, by providing the objectives and goals against
which performance can be measured and evaluated.

Once the plan has been developed, we have established the mission the organization
seeks to attain as well as specific key result areas and related objectives and goals
which must be achieved. These provide focus for people's decisions and actions.

ENDNOTES

25. For more discussion on goals and objectives and their impact on performance, see:
Chesney, A.A. and E.A. Locke, 1991, "Relationships Among Goal Difficulty, Business Strategies, and Performance on a Complex Management Simulation Task", <u>Academy of Management Journal</u>, 34: 162-193.
Erez, M., P.C. Earley, and C.L. Hulin, 1985, "Impact of Participation on Goal Acceptance and Performance: a Two-Step Model", <u>Academy of Management Journal</u>, 28: 50-66.
Earley, P.C., T. Connolly, and G. Ekegren, 1989, "Goals, Strategy Development, and Task Performance: Some Limits on the Efficacy of Goal Setting", <u>Journal of Applied Psychology</u>, 74: 24-33.
26. For research on the relationship of goals and motivation see:
Shalley, C.E., G.R. Oldham, and J.F. Porac, 1987, "Effects of Goal Difficulty, Goal-Setting Method, and Expected External Evaluation on Intrinsic Motivation", <u>Academy of Management Journal</u>: 30: 553-563.
Shalley, C.E. and G.R. Oldham, 1985, "Effects of Goal Difficulty and Expected External Evaluation on Intrinsic Motivation: A Laboratory Study", <u>Academy of Management Journal</u>: 28: 628-640.
Tubbs, M.E. and S.E. Ekeberg, 1991, "The Role of Intentions in Work Motivation: Implications for Goal-Setting Theory and Research", <u>Academy of Management Review</u>, 16: 188-199.
Sullivan, J., 1988, "Three Roles of Language in Motivation Theory", <u>Academy of Management Review</u>, 13, 104-115.
27. For research on the relationship between goals and control, see:
Green, S.E. and M.A. Welsh, 1988, "Cybernetics and Dependence: Reframing the Control Concept", <u>Academy of Management Review</u>, 13, 287-301.

REFERENCES

Chesney, A.A. and E.A. Locke, 1991, "Relationships Among Goal Difficulty, Business Strategies, and Performance on a Complex Management Simulation Task", Academy of Management Journal, 34: 162-193.

Earley, P.C., T. Connolly, and G. Ekegren, 1989, "Goals, Strategy Development, and Task Performance: Some Limits on the Efficacy of Goal Setting", Journal of Applied Psychology, 74: 24-33.

Erez, M., P.C. Earley, and C.L. Hulin, 1985, "Impact of Participation on Goal Acceptance and Performance: a Two-Step Model", Academy of Management Journal, 28: 50-66.

Green, S.E. and M.A. Welsh, 1988, "Cybernetics and Dependence: Reframing the Control Concept", Academy of Management Review, 13, 287-301.

Shalley, C.E. and G.R. Oldham, 1985, "Effects of Goal Difficulty and Expected External Evaluation on Intrinsic Motivation: A Laboratory Study", Academy of Management Journal: 28: 628-640.

Shalley, C.E., G.R. Oldham, and J.F. Porac, 1987, "Effects of Goal Difficulty, Goal-Setting Method, and Expected External Evaluation on Intrinsic Motivation", Academy of Management Journal: 30: 553-563.

Sullivan, J., 1988, "Three Roles of Language in Motivation Theory", Academy of Management Review, 13, 104-115.

Tubbs, M.E. and S.E. Ekeberg, 1991, "The Role of Intentions in Work Motivation: Implications for Goal-Setting Theory and Research", Academy of Management Review, 16: 188-199.

4

THE ROLE OF MEASUREMENT
AND FEEDBACK IN CONTROL

This chapter examines the role of "measurement" and "feedback" in organizational control.[28] We shall develop a framework for viewing the measurement and feedback as components of a core control system from the perspective of attempts to influence human behavior, rather than to merely represent things in numerical terms. The framework is termed the "Psycho-Technical Systems" (or PTS) model of measurement.[29]

NATURE OF MEASUREMENT AND FEEDBACK

It is important to recognize that there are different concepts of the raison d'etre of measurement. Three alternative concepts of the purpose of measurement are:

1. measurement as an end in itself;
2. measurement as a means to an end (indirect effect on behavior); and
3. measurement as a direct-effect on behavior.

Each of these notions are examined below in the context of a discussion of the prevailing measurement paradigm as well as the PTS model.

Traditional Measurement Paradigm

The traditional and currently prevailing paradigm of measurement treats it as a technology for representing the properties (or qualities) of objects in numerical terms.[30] Typifying this view, Stevens states that "measurement is the assignment of numerals to objects or events according to rules."[31] Campbell defines measurement as "...the process of assigning numbers to represent qualities."[32] Also Grove, Mock, and Ehrenreich state: "The primary purpose of measurement is the establishment of empirical rules of correspondence between a set of empirical objects (A) and a set of numerals (N). The numerals act as surrogates for relevant attributes as the measurement objects."[33]

All of the definitions of measurement presented above are representational concepts; that is, they treat measurement as a technology for representing the properties of objects in numerical terms. Stated differently, traditional representation has been the raison d'etre of measurement.

Different interpretations can be made of the extent to which the raison d'etre underlying the traditional paradigm is "measurement as an end in itself" or "measurement as a means to an end." In physical science, we may be concerned with measuring some phenomenon such as the speed of light either as an end in itself simply because it is an aspect of nature, or as a means toward some specified end. In effect, there is merely a difference in the degree to which a purpose for the measurement has been specified, and this may vary from a very tenuous specification to one that is much more precise. Thus we can view these notions of raison d'etre as points on a continuum, rather than as discrete classes, as shown in Figure 4-1.

In accounting in the U.S. prior to the 1960's, the prevailing measurement paradigm treated accounting measurement between points (A) and (B) on the continuum shown in Figure 4-1, that is, it tended to be viewed somewhere between an end in itself and as a means to an end. More specifically, it was intended to represent economic transactions per se rather than necessarily be useful for decisions. This is analogous to the measurement of temperature in physical sciences. This can be used as a general purpose measurement with specific uses unspecified, or for a very well defined purpose.

Behavioral influence as the Raison d'etre of Organizational Measurement

The raison d'etre of organizational measurement systems is to influence the behavior of people: their perceptions, motivation, and, ultimately decisions and actions. The concept of "behavioral influence" posited here for organizational measurement systems is qualitatively different from merely stating that measurement is intended to be useful. The present argument is that the ultimate purpose of measurement is to influence behavior. This implies that a measurement technology must be viewed as and designed as a mechanism to effect behavior rather than to represent the properties of objects in numerical terms. Thus this concept of measurement as a mechanism to influence behavior is compatible with the intended role of measurement as part of an organizational control system.

This alternative concept of the role of measurement in organizations has been evolving for many years; but it has neither been explicitly accepted as the basis of a new paradigm of organizational measurement, nor has it been developed into a formal model with premises, propositions, and criteria. In brief, a meta-theory of measurement based upon the notion of behavioral influence does not yet exist.

In previous research, an attempt was made to formulate the basic ideas of the alternative behavioral model of measurement. This meta-theory of measurement was termed a "Psycho-technical Systems" (PTS) approach.[34]

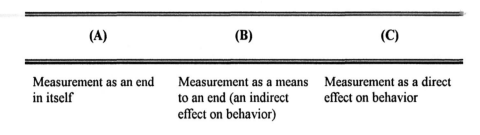

(A)	(B)	(C)
Measurement as an end in itself	Measurement as a means to an end (an indirect effect on behavior)	Measurement as a direct effect on behavior

Figure 4-1
Continuum of Notions of
Raison d'etre Underlying Measurement

The PTS model is based upon the notion that the principal difference between measurement systems used in organizations ("organizational measurement systems") and those developed for use in physical science is the degree to which the former are intended to have functions other than merely representation of objects in numerical terms. Organizational measurement systems are typically intended to perform a representational function not as an end in itself, but rather, as a means of ultimately influencing human behavior. This point is illustrated systematically in Figure 4-2. As shown in Figure 4-2, both physical science and organizational measurement require representation as well as direct behavioral effect. But they differ in the degree or proportion of these desired properties.

THE PSYCHO-TECHNICAL SYSTEMS FRAMEWORK

This section examines the framework of measurement as a psycho-technical system. It deals with the structure of the framework and the concepts of measurement which underlie it.

Measurement as a Psycho-Technical System

The term "psycho-technical system" is used here to refer to any technology that is intended to perform or effect certain predefined psychological (behavioral) functions. The term "technology" as it is used here means something different from machine technology. It is used in the sense proposed by Jaques Ellul and refers to any complex of standardized means for attaining a predetermined result.[35] Thus, a psycho-technical measurement system is intended to perform certain predefined psychological (behavioral) functions through the process and output of measurement.

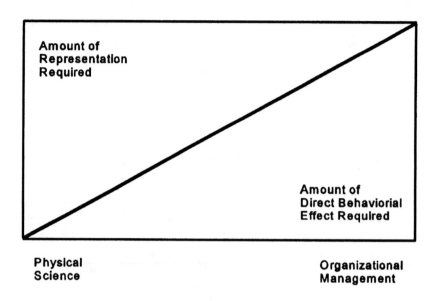

Figure 4-2
Relation Between Amounts of Representation and
Direct Behavioral Effect Required on
Physical Science and Organizations

The PTS model is based on the notion that the principal purpose of measurement in organizations is to influence human behavior. Under this model, behavior is the end result of measurement. Accordingly, this presupposes that the designers of an organizational measurement system have a concept of the desired behavioral outcomes their systems are intended to produce. This requires, in turn, that the design of organizational measurement systems must be based upon a blueprint of expected behaviors. At present, we must admit that the technology to blueprint expected behaviors form measurement systems is not well developed; this is an area for future research.

Domains of Measurement

In the context of human organizations, there are three domains of measurements: (1) the sender's behavior, (2) the receiver's behavior, and (3) the phenomenon being measured. The "sender" refers to the person(s) required to measure some object or phenomenon. The "receiver" refers to the person(s) who receive measurements. The "phenomenon" being measured refers to the object to which the rules of measurement are applied.

Prior research has not explicitly recognized and developed a total systems view of the effects of the act of measurement; rather, recognition of its significance has been in bits and pieces. For example, Prakash & Rappaport have examined the effects of the act of measurement upon the information sender, but not upon the information receiver or the phenomenon being measured itself.[36] In addition, most studies recognizing the effects of the act of measurement upon receivers have viewed the phenomenon as an aberration, rather than as a normal inherent part of the measurement process.

Elements of Measurement

A basic premise underlying the PTS framework is that there are two major elements of measurement: (1) the numbers produced by a measurement system and (2) the act or measurement itself.

The numbers produced by measurement are the outputs of the measurement system. They are typically intended to provide information for decision-making or evaluation (feedback). They are an important element, but not the only element, or measurement.

The second element of measurement is the process or act of measurement per se. The very act of measuring some object or phenomenon may have certain functions in the context of organizations.

Figure 4-3 shows schematically the relation between the domains and elements of measurement. Under the PTS concept, we are concerned about a dual aspect of the effect of measurement: (1) the effects of the measurement process or act of measurement upon the phenomenon measured per se and (2) the effects of the output of the measurement system, the numbers produced, upon all three domains of measurement.

These two aspects of measurement have different functions or purposes in influencing human behavior. The former are termed "process functions" or measurement, while the latter may be termed "output functions." Process functions are the functions performed by the act of measurement, while output functions are the functions performed by the numbers produced by measurement.

Measurement Elements	Measurement Domains		
	Sender	Receiver	Phenomena Measured
Output			
Process			

Figure 4-3
Relation Between Domains and Elements

Each of these two elements of measurement (process and output) have different subfunctions. The process element of measurement (the act of measurement) performs four basic functions: (1) the criterion function, (2) the catalyst function, (3) the set function and (4) the motivational function. These four process functions of measurement, shown schematically in Figure 4-4, are described in the subsequent section. The output element of measurement (the numbers provided by measurement) has two basic functions: (1) information for decision making, and (2) information for feedback (evaluative feedback and corrective feedback). These two output functions of measurement, shown schematically in Figure 4-4, are examined below.

MEASUREMENT'S PROCESS FUNCTIONS

The intended purpose of measurement systems is to influence various aspects of the process of management--decision making, planning, and control.

The measurement process can influence management behavior through a variety of ways. Four principal ways (or subfunctions of the measurement process) have been identified in Figure 4-4, and each of these subfunctions is described, in turn, below.

The Criterion Function

A principal process function of measurement systems is to provide an "operational criterion" or set of criteria to guide decisions. This means that a measurement system operationally defines the goal of an activity.

The accounting measurement system performs the criterion function by "coding" economic transactions and events into a "bottom line." As Katz & Kahn state: "Through the coding process the 'blooming, buzzing, confusion' of the world is simplified into a few meaningful categories for a given system."[37]

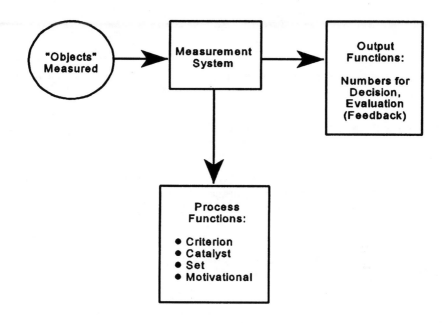

Figure 4-4
Elements of Measurement

There are three psychological effects of a measurement-system-defined performance criterion. First, it tends to provide a focus or direction for efforts. Second, it helps structure thought and analysis. Third, it provides a model of the relevant set of variables to which effort ought to be directed.

The role of the measurement system as a model of the decision maker's "world" may be better appreciated by drawing upon the work of Piaget. In discussing Piaget's ideas, Carroll states that:[38]

"The unifying theme in the work of Piaget is the gradual unfolding of the individual's ability to construct an internal "model" of the universe around him and to perform manipulations on that model so as to draw conclusions about the probable past history of his environment as the probable results of possible actions that could be taken upon that environment. The ability to do this is the essence of all "thinking" in the non-trivial meaning of the term."

Thus, the measurement system provides an implicit model or set of criteria through which the decision maker organizes thought.

The need for such structured thought is derived from limits on man's cognitive information-processing capacities.[39] The psychological role of the criterion function is thus to provide mechanisms to simplify cognitive information-processing requirements.

Another way of looking at the criterion function is that it performs the "coding" process described by Katz and Kahn.[40]

Criterion Function in Human-Resource Management

We can illustrate the role of the criterion function in the context of human-resource management, which, to a very great extent, consists of decision making. Management continuously makes decisions involving the acquisition, development, allocation, and compensation of human resources. For example, since people differ in such qualities as intelligence, skills, motivation, and personality, management must decide what qualities are desirable in people recruited into a firm. It must also evaluate possible job candidates and select people. Similarly, management must decide how to allocate its existing people to roles. It must also decide if the firm should invest in specialized training programs.

Such human-resource management decisions should be based upon some guiding criterion or standard. This means that there should be a measure of a decision's potential consequences for an organization. In other words, what is the utility of this decision for an organization? In addition, it would help if all decisions could be based upon a common criterion so that they could be compared. Unfortunately while the logic of this approach may be obvious, it is typically not feasible to apply it to human-resource decision because of the lack of a well-defined conception of the ultimate goal of such decisions.

The development of Human Resource Accounting (HRA) measures is, in part, based on the recognition of the need for such a criterion.[41] The criterion suggested by HRA is a person's value to an organization. For example in Human-resource-acquisition decisions, the criterion used in selecting people should be the expected value of people to the organization. Similarly, in human-resource-development decisions, the criterion should be the expected increase in human-resource value, as reflected in the return on investment. In addition, in deciding whom to retain in layoff decisions, the criterion should be the relative value of people to the enterprise. These examples are intended to be illustrative and not exhaustive.

These measures of human-resource value define the goals of human resource management activity even if the measures themselves are difficult to operationalize or the measurements derived are subject to error. Their function is to provide a criterion to guide decisions as much as to provide measurements of the criterion per se. Thus it would be incorrect to apply the traditional criteria for representational validity and reliability to evaluate proposed measures of human-resource value because such measures may perform the criterion function irrespective of their degree of representational validity or reliability.

Another example of the criterion function of measurements is provided by Mirvis and Lawler.[42] They argue that while the behavioral literature contains a large number of studies of the relationship between attitudes and absenteeism, turnover, tardiness, job performance, strikes, and grievances, no study has measured the costs associated with different levels of job satisfaction and motivation. "Thus, psychologists are still unable to talk in dollars and cents when they argue for measuring employee attitudes and for improving job satisfaction." Measurements of human resource costs, in spite of errors of estimates, would permit a monetary criterion to be applied to such analyses. Again, the function of measurement is to provide the criterion as well as the measurements (numbers) per se.

The Catalyst Function

A second process function of measurement is to serve as a "catalyst" to produce systematic planning. The process of measurement causes systematic consideration of the parameters which underlie the derived measurement.

The catalyst function of the act of measurement is related to what Prakash and Rappaport have termed "information inductance." As they state: "Information inductance is the process whereby the behavior of an individual is affected by the information he is required to communicate."[43] Similarly, measurement serves as a catalyst to cause an individual to consider the variables which are inputs to the measurement process.

The effects of the catalyst function can be illustrated in the context of operational budgeting. Budgets involve forecasts of future parameters (costs, revenues, production rates, etc.). Consequently, there may be a great degree of certainty in the numbers derived from the budgeting process. However, through the process of measuring the parameters included in a budget, managers may be caused to consider the effects of those variables. This is especially true for the case of multiplan (flexible) budgeting. Thus the calculation or measurement of variables in a budget is a catalyst to systematic operational planning.

Catalyst Function in Human-Resources Management

In the context of human-resource management, the process of measuring human-resource value is also intended to function as a catalyst to produce systematic planning of human resources. In the process of measuring human-resource value, managers are forced to think systematically about human resources. They must project future requirements for people and the tasks they may perform and assess the value of these tasks to the organization. They must also assess the supply of people anticipated to be available, the probabilities that these people will occupy various positions, their need for training and development to enhance promotability, their transferability, and the likelihood that they will remain in the firm. Thus, in the measurement of human-resource value, the numbers produced may not be as important as the process that must be employed to derive those numbers. This suggests that subjectivity involved in measuring such contrasts as human-resource value may not be a critical limitation; for even though the numbers derived may be uncertain, the measurement process may cause systematic planning to occur.

The Set Function

Another function of measurement systems is to influence the "set" of managers who engaged in decision making. The term "set" refers to a cognitive expectation of what a decision maker is "ready" to perceive. Measurement can influence a decision maker's set by providing information about relevant variables to be considered. Thus they can influence the variables or criteria used in decision making. They very act of measuring and reporting a certain informational cue can cause it to be considered rather than ignored in a decision making process.

Set Function in Human-Resource Management

In human-resource management, measurements can be used to influence the decision maker's set.[44] For example, there is a tendency for decisions to be made without consideration of their effects upon a person's value to the organization. Decisions tend to be made on the basis of short-term benefits and costs, and not with respect to their longer term consequences for the value of human resources.

The Motivational Function

A fourth process of measurement is to influence both the direction and magnitude of motivation. The motivational function is closely related to the set function. The presence or absence of measurement of an object or activity influences motivation independently of the numbers which are derived.

The measurement process functions as a motivational mechanism because it is linked (or at least perceived so) to the organizational reward system. Ijiri illustrates how a measurement system may influence motivation:[45]

> "Another way an accounting system determines the goals for a manager is by defining an area for himself to pay attention to. For example, assume the accountants suddenly report scrap cost for the first time. The manager now creates a goal that specifies his objectives in regard to the control for scrap cost..."

Although the process is not quite so direct, the act of measurement may lead to changes in the direction of motivation. As Ridgeway states: "Even where performance measures are instituted purely for purposes of information, they are probably interpreted as definitions of the important aspects of their job or activity and hence have important implications of the motivation of behavior."[46]

The hypothesized effects of the motivational function of measurement have been studied empirically. For example, Cammann found that managers concentrated their efforts on areas where the results were measured.[47]

Motivational Function in Human-Resource Management

The measurement process can also play a motivational role in the content of the human-resource management process. For example, measures of human-resource value may be used to motivate human-resource development and conservation. If the value of human resources under a manager's stewardship is measured, we anticipate that the manager will pay attention to, and be concerned about, changes in human-resource value. For example, if one factor used in evaluating the performance of managing partners in local CPA firm offices is the change in human-resource value attributable to development, we may expect that a greater degree of attention will be devoted to the development process. The manager may begin to ask himself: "How can I utilize this person in a way that will enhance his value to the firm?" Thus the measurement process rather than the numbers per se influence the decisions of managers in this situation.

Relations Among Process Functions

The four process functions examined above are closely related. Intuitively, they may be viewed as comprising two different dimensions. The first type of dimension (type 1) is the criterion function, and the second (type 2) is the other three functions: catalyst, set, and motivational.

Type 1 is concerned with providing a focus for thought and analysis. Is provides and operational goal to guide decisions. Type 2 are all concerned with different aspects of influencing behavior. They may be viewed as different degrees of effect on behavior as shown in Figure 4-5.

PTS Criteria For Process Functions of Management

Given the present function of measurement as a representational system, the traditional criteria of validity and reliability are appropriate to evaluate the representational properties of numbers.

Type 1 Process Functions		Process Function Description	Degree of Effect on Behavior
(1)	Set	A means of influencing perception	Weak
(2)	Catalyst	A means of inducing systematic thought	Semi-Strong
(3)	Motivational	A means of influencing action or decisions	Strong

Figure 4-5
Degrees of Effect of
Type 1 Process Functions on Behavior

The traditional notion of "validity" refers to the extent a measurement represents what it purports to represent. "Reliability" refers to the reproductability of the measurement. Both of these constructs are representational constructs.

With a shift to a PTS concept of measurement based upon recognition of the functions of the measurement process, the traditional criteria are insufficient (and perhaps sometimes irrelevant). Instead, a different set of criteria are required which are based upon the PTS view.

Two tentative PTS measurement criteria have been proposed which are relevant here: (1) behavioral validity and (2) behavioral reliability.[48] "Behavioral validity" refers to the extent to which a measurement process leads to the behaviors it is intended to produce. It does not concern itself with the issue of whether the measure represents the object being measured in a valid way; but, rather, whether the intended effects (or behaviors) occur. "Behavioral reliability" refers to the extent to which the behavioral outcomes produced by the measurement process are consistently produced. It does not concern itself with the representational reliability of measures. In principle, the constructs of behavioral validity and reliability are independent. A measurement system may lead to behaviors it purports to lead to, but do so unreliably. Alternatively, it may lead to invalid (unintended) behaviors quite consistently.

A behaviorally valid measure is one that leads to intended consequences and the degree of behavioral validity is the extent to which this occurs. For example, the behavioral purpose of a measurement system may be to motivate managers to pay attention to human resource development as well as to current productivity. It may not be possible to develop a measure of personnel development with a high degree of representational validity. Yet it may be possible to construct a measure that has behavioral validity, because by simply measuring employee development in some manner decision-maker may be motivated to increase it (the motivational function). The measure's behavioral reliability is the extent to which it consistently produces concern for employee development.

In brief, the basic argument here is that the different purposes of measurement require different criteria. The weight placed upon behavioral criteria is greater than upon representational criteria when the purpose of measurement is direct behavioral influence, and vice versa. This is shown schematically in Figure 4-6.

Purposes of Measurement	Types of Criteria			
	Presentation		Behavioral	
	Validity	Reliability	Validity	Reliability
(1) Representation	High	Low	Low	Low
(2) Behavioral Influence	Low	Low	High	High

* High = High degree of weight on criterion.
  Low = Low degree of weight on criterion.

Figure 4-6
Different Measurement Criteria Weights for
Different Measurement Purposes

Measurement's Medium As Its Message

The prior analysis of the subfunctions of the measurement process has been based on the notion of measurement as a PTS. It has been proposed that the measurement process has certain built-in psychological functions for decision makers.

An alternative explanation of the psychological effects of measurement system can be found in the thought of Marshall McLuhan.[49] Drawing upon McLuhan, one can argue that the medium of measurement is its message. The very fact that an organization is measuring some object may convey a meaning to people in an organization beyond the numbers derived from the measurement system. This means that the measurement process is itself part of the stimulus as well as the measurements produced.

In the context of human-resource management, an experiment by Schwan suggests how measurements of investments in human resources may convey a meaning to decision makers (investors) beyond the numbers generated as the output of that measurement process.[50] Schwan provided two sets of financial statements to managers and analysts employed in investment, credit, and trust departments of nine large banks. In Set A, human resource costs were treated as a period cost (expensed as incurred), while in Set B they were treated as assets. Subjects were required to rate the management of the firms and to make predictions of operating revenues and income. Subjects were also asked an open-ended question about the reasons for their ratings of management.

Their responses to the question suggest that the very fact that "firm B" was measuring investment in human resources had an effect on the subjects' decision processes. It led to different perceptions of the firms and their managements. Some of the subjects specifically referred to human resources as reasons for their judgments of management and noted that the firm measuring human resources was "more progressive."

MEASUREMENT'S OUTPUT FUNCTIONS

The intended purpose of measurement is to influence management planning, decision-making, and control. The numerical output of the measurement process can influence management behavior in a variety of ways.

Two principal ways (or subfunctions of measurement's output function) can be identified: (1) the decision-making function, and (2) the feedback function. Each of these subfunctions are well-known in management literature, and, therefore, will be discussed only briefly below.

The Decision-Making Function

A principal function of measurement systems is to provide information to guide decisions. This means that a measurement system generates numbers which are intended to be useful in management decision-making. Thus it implies that measurement is intended to <u>influence</u> decisions behavior through the numbers it provides. Indeed, this is one major aspect of the informational functions we typically associate with measurement systems. For example, the accounting system is a measurement system designed to provide financial information for management decision-making.

The Feedback Function

A second major subfunction of the output function of measurement systems is to provide "feedback," or information about the results of operations and activities.[51]

As discussed in Chapter 3, there are two types of feedback information: (1) corrective feedback and (2) evaluative feedback. The former provides information for the adjustment of operations in order to confirm more closely to plan, while the latter provides information to be used in assessing the quality of performance. This latter function shall be examined in Chapter 5.

CONCLUSION

This chapter has examined the role of measurement and feedback in control. The framework of measurement adopted here is based upon the notion that measurement process is a "psycho-technical system," a technology designed to influence human behavior, rather than merely a representational technology.

According to the PTS model, measurement has two basic elements: (1) the numbers produced and (2) the act of measurement itself. The numbers produced are the outputs of the measurement system and perform two subfunctions: a) they provide information for decision-making, and b) feedback information for performance evaluation. The act of measurement itself, termed measurement's process function, performed four related subfunctions; it serves as: a) a criterion for decision-making, b) a catalyst for systematic planning, c) a way of influencing a decision-makers set, and d) a mechanism for motivating attention to relevant performance (or result) areas.

A measurement subsystem plays a vital role in the functioning of an overall core control system. This chapter has examined the dynamics of how measurement and feedback (viewed as a component of measurement) functions as part of the overall core control system as well as an independent operating system.

ENDNOTES

28. For a more detailed discussion of various aspects of feedback, see:
    Ashford, S.J. and A.S. Tsui, 1991, "Self Regulation for Managerial Effectiveness: The Role of Active Feedback Seeking:, Academy of Management Journal, 34: 251-280.
    Baron, Robert A., 1990," Countering the Effects of Destructive Criticism: The Relative Efficiency of Four Interventions", Journal of Applied Psychology, 75: 235-245.
    Earley, P.C., G.B. Nortcraft, C. Lee, T.R. Lituchy, 1990, "The Impact of Process and Outcome Feedback on the Relation of Goal Setting to Task Performance", Academy of Management Journal, 33: 87-105.
    Hedge, J.W. and M.J. Kavanagh, 1988, "Improving the Accuracy of Performance Evaluations: Comparison of Three Methods of Performance Appraiser Training", Journal of Applied Psychology, 73: 68-73.
    Klein, J.I., 1990 "Feasibility Theory: A Resource-Munificence Model of Work Motivation and Behavior", Academy of Management Review, 15: 646-665.
    Matsui, T., T. Kakuyama, and M.L.U. Onglato, 1987, "Effects of Goal and Feedback on Performance in Groups", Journal of Applied Psychology, 72: 407-425.
    Vance, R.J. and A Colella, 1990, "Effects of Two Types of Feedback on Goal Acceptance and Personal Goals", Journal of Applied Psychology, 75: 68-76.
29. This chapter draws upon Eric G. Flamholtz's, "Towards a Psycho-Technical Systems Paradigm of Organizational Measurement," Decision Sciences, January 1979, pp. 71-84. As examined below, this chapter treats feedback as an element of measurement: specifically, as part of the output function of measurement. The "representational" aspects of measurement are treated in chapter 5 as part of the "measurement aspects of evaluation."
30. As Ijiri states: "...measurement is an assignment m of numbers to objects p with the intent that is given a k-tuple of numbers assigned to them $<m(p1), m(p2),...., m(pk)>$ is in the surrogate relations, and if $<p1, p2,...., pk>$ is not in the surrogate relation."
    Ijiri, Yuji, Theory of Accounting Measurement, Studies in Accounting, Research No. 10, Sarasorta, FL: American Accounting Association, 1975, p. 42.
31. Stevens, S.S., "On The Theory of Scales of Measurement," Science, 1946, p. 667.
32. Campbell, N.R., Foundations of Science, New York, NY: Dover Publications, 1957, p. 267.
33. Grove, H.T., Mock, J. and Ehrenreich, K., "A Review of HRA Measurement Systems from a Measurement Theory Perspective," Accounting Organizations and Society, 1977, p. 219.
34. Flamholtz, Eric, "Toward a Psycho-Technical Systems Paradigm of Organizational Measurement," Decision Sciences, January, 1979, pp. 71-84.
35. Ellul, J., The Technological Society, New York: Alfred A. Knopf, 1964.
36. Prakash, P. and Rappaport, A., "Information Inductance and Its Significance For Accounting, Accounting, Organizations and Society, 1977, pp. 29-38.
37. Katz, D. and Kahn, R.L., The Social Psychology of Organizations, New York, NY: John Wiley and Sons, 1966, p. 22.
38. Carroll, J.B., Language and Thought, Englewood Cliffs, NJ: Prentice-Hall, Inc., 1964, p. 79.
39. Gardner, W.R., "Attention: The Processing of Multiple Sources of Information," Handbook of Perception, Vol. II: Psychophysical Judgement and Measurement, Edited by E. Carterette and M. Friedman. New York: Academic Press, 1974, pp. 23-24.
40. Katz, D. and Kahn, R.L., The Social Psychology of Organizations, New York, NY: John Wiley and Sons, 1966, p. 22.
41. Flamholtz, Eric, "Toward a Psycho-Technical Systems Paradigm of Organizational Measurement," Decision Sciences, January, 1979, pp. 71-84.
42. Mirvis, P.H. and Lawler, E.E., "Measuring the Financial Impact of Employee Attitudes," Journal of Applied Psychology, Vol. 62, No. 2, 1977, pp. 1-8.
43. Prakash, P. and Rappaport, A., "Information Inductance and Its Significance For Accounting," Accounting, Organizations and Society, 1977, p. 29.

44. This research study suggests how the presence or absence of human-resource value (HRV) measures can influence a decision maker's set. In this study, using a test-retest design, decision makers were asked to choose between two individuals for a job assignment (allocations) in a CPA firm. In the first test, they were presented with traditional performance appraisal data on which to base decisions. The decision makers were also asked to indicate their reasons for their choice. Their responses were content-analyzed and found to be primarily concerned with the relative capabilities of value of the people to either (1) serve the firm's current needs or (2) serve the needs of the client. They did not consider the needs of the individuals assigned or the effect of the anticipated assignment on their value to the firm. In the second test, they were presented with nonmonetary human-resource valuation data. Specifically, they received estimates of assessments of the expected promotability of the staff and the probability that they would remain in the firm. The rationale for these decisions was also content analyzed, and the results indicated that a significantly greater percentage of the reasons concerned the effect of the job assignment upon the individual's value to the firm than to either serve the firm's or client's needs. The third retest presented the subject with monetary data about the individual's expected value. The content analysis indicated a significant change in the set used to reach the decision. In brief, the presence of the HRV measures stimulated a different way of thinking about the decisions; there was a change in the proportion of people using each factor to select each staff accountant for the job assignment from the first to second to third tests.
45. Ijiri, Yuji, The Foundations of Accounting Measurement, Englewood Cliffs, NJ: Prentice-Hall, Inc., 1967, p. 158.
46. Ridgeway, V.F., "Dysfunctional Consequences of Performance Measurements," Administrative Science Quarterly, September, 1956, p. 247.
47. Cammann, C., "The Impact of a Feedback System on Managerial Attitudes and Performance," Unpublished Ph.D. dissertation, Yale University, 1974.
48. Flamholtz, Eric, "Toward a Psycho-Technical Systems Paradigm of Organizational Measurement," Decision Sciences, January, 1979, pp. 82-83.
49. McLuhan, M., Understanding Media: The Extensions of Man, New York: McGraw-Hill Book Company, 1964.
50. Schwan, E.S., "The Effects of Human Resource Accounting Data on Financial Decisions: An Empirical Test," Accounting, Organizations and Society, 1976, pp. 219-238.
51. For a more detailed discussion of various aspects of feedback, see:
    Ashford, S.J. and A.S. Tsui, 1991, "Self Regulation for Managerial Effectiveness: The Role of Active Feedback Seeking", Academy of Management Journal, 34: 251-280.
    Baron, Robert A., 1990, "Countering the Effects of Destructive Criticism: The Relative Efficacy of Four Interventions", Journal of Applied Psychology, 75: 235-245.
    Earley, P.C., G.B. Northcraft, C. Lee, T.R. Lituchy, 1990, "The Impact of Process and Outcome Feedback on the Relation of Goal Setting to Task Performance", Academy of Management Journal, 33, 87-105.
    Hedge, J.W. and M.J. Kavanagh, 1988, "Improving the Accuracy of Performance Evaluations: Comparison of Three Methods of Performance Appraiser Training", Journal of Applied Psychology, 73: 68-73.
    Klein, J.I., 1990, "Feasibility Theory: A Resource-Munificence Model of Work Motivation and Behavior", Academy of Management Review, 15: 646-665.
    Matsui, T., T. Kakuyama, and M.L.U. Onglato, 1987, "Effects of Goals and Feedback on Performance in Groups", Journal of Applied Psychology, 72: 407-415.
    Vance, R.J. and A. Colella, 1990, "Effects of Two Types of Feedback on Goal Acceptance and Personal Goals, Journal of Applied Psychology, 75: 68-76.

REFERENCES

Ashford, S.J. and A.S. Tsui, 1991, "Self Regulation for Managerial Effectiveness: The Role of Active Feedback Seeking", Academy of Management Journal, 34: 251-280.

Baron, Robert A., 1990, "Countering the Effects of Destructive Criticism: The Relative Efficacy of Four Interventions", Journal of Applied Psychology, 75: 235-245.

Birnberg, J.G. and Snodgrass, C., "Culture and Control: A Field Study," Accounting, Organizations and Society, Vol. 13, No. 5, 1988, pp. 447-464.

Cammann, C., "The Impact of a Feedback System on Managerial Attitudes and Performance," Unpublished Ph.D. dissertation, Yale University, 1974.

Campbell, N.R., Foundations of Science, New York, NY: Dover Publications, 1957.

Carroll, J.B., Language and Thought, Englewood Cliffs, NJ: Prentice-Hall, Inc., 1964.

Earley, P.C., G.B. Northcraft, C. Lee, T.R. Lituchy, 1990, "The Impact of Process and Outcome Feedback on the Relation of Goal Setting to Task Performance", Academy of Management Journal, 33, 87-105.

Eisenhardt, K.M., "Control: Organizational and Economic Approaches," Management Science, Vol. 31, 1985, pp. 134-149.

Ellul, J., The Technological Society, New York: Alfred A. Knopf, 1964.

Flamholtz, Eric, Growing Pains: How To Make The Transition From Entrepreneurship to a Professionally Managed Firm, San Francisco, CA: Jossey-Bass Publishers, Inc., 1990.

Flamholtz, Eric, Human Resource Accounting, San Francisco, CA: Jossey-Bass Publishers, Inc., 1985.

Flamholtz, Eric, "Toward a Psycho-Technical Systems Paradigm of Organizational Measurement," Decision Sciences (January, 1979), pp. 71-84.

Gardner, W.R., "Attention: The Processing of Multiple Sources of Information," Handbook of Perception, Vol. II: Psychophysical Judgement and Measurement, Edited by E. Carterette and M. Friedman. New York: Academic Press, 1974, pp. 23-59.

Grove, H.T., Mock, J. and Ehrenreich, K., "A Review of HRA Measurement Systems from a Measurement Theory Perspective," Accounting Organizations and Society, 1977, pp. 219-236.

Hedge, J.W. and M.J. Kavanagh, 1988, "Improving the Accuracy of Performance Evaluations: Comparison of Three Methods of Performance Appraiser Training", Journal of Applied Psychology, 73: 68-73.

Ijiri, Yuji, Theory of Accounting Measurement, Studies in Accounting, Research No. 10, Sarasota, FL: American Accounting Association, 1975.

Katz, D. & Kahn, R.L., The Social Psychology of Organizations, New York, NY: John Wiley and Sons, 1966.

Klein, J.I., 1990, "Feasibility Theory: A Resource-Munificence Model of Work Motivation and Behavior", Academy of Management Review, 15: 646-665.

Matsui, T., T. Kakuyama, and M.L.U. Onglato, 1987, "Effects of Goals and Feedback on Performance in Groups", Journal of Applied Psychology, 72: 407-415.

McLuhan, M., Understanding Media: The Extensions of Man, New York: McGraw-Hill Book Company, 1964.

Mirvis, P.H. and Lawler, E.E., "Measuring the Financial Impact of Employee Attitudes," Journal of Applied Psychology, Vol. 62, No. 2, 1977, pp. 1-8.

Mock, T.J., Measurement and Accounting Information Criteria, Studies in Accounting, Research No. 13, Sarasota, FL: American Accounting Association, 1976.

Prakash, P. and Rappaport, A., "Information Inductance and Its Significance For Accounting, Accounting, Organizations and Society, 1977, pp. 29-38.

Ridgeway, V.F., "Dysfunctional Consequences of Performance Measurements," Administrative Science Quarterly, September, 1956, pp. 240-247.

Schwan, E.S., "The Effects of Human Resource Accounting Data on Financial Decisions: An Empirical Test," Accounting, Organizations and Society, 1976, pp. 219-238.

Stevens, S.S., "On The Theory of Scales of Measurement," Science, 1946, pp. 667-680.

Vance, R.J. and A. Colella, 1990, "Effects of Two Types of Feedback on Goal Acceptance and Personal Goals, Journal of Applied Psychology, 75: 68-76.

Williamson, O.E., The Economic Institutions of Capitalism, New York: Free Press, 1985.

5

THE ROLE OF EVALUATION IN ORGANIZATIONAL CONTROL

The "evaluation and reward subsystem" refers to the component systems of the overall core control systems (shown in Figure 2-2) which deals with the process of assessing human performance and rewarding it. The evaluation system concerns the assessment of the quality of performance and provides the basis for administration of rewards. Thus these two systems individually and in combination play a crucial role in the overall process of organizational control.[52] Although the merging of the evaluation and reward processes of an organization creates a system per se, we shall first examine each of these two processes as independent systems.

This chapter examines the nature of the evaluation subsystem and several aspects of its role in organizational control. We shall:

1. Examine the nature of the evaluation system;
2. Identify its functions as a component part of the core control system;
3. Examine the different types of methods of evaluation systems; and
4. Consider the problems of evaluation in organizational control.

Thus this chapter shall examine what happens in the evaluation component of the evaluation-reward system's box of the core control model shown in Figure 2-2.

NATURE OF EVALUATION SYSTEM

The process of evaluation in an organization is one of the most complex, demanding, and important functions facing a manager and an organization.[53] Why? Because it determines how people are "valued" by an organization which, in turn, influences and individual's own self perception of his or her own self-worth as well as the financial and nonfinancial rewards the person is likely to receive.

To the extent that an organization's evaluations affect either a person's perceived self-worth or rewards provided to the individual, the evaluation process becomes inextricably linked to the ability of people to satisfy their needs. This means that evaluation plays a critical role in both Ex Ante and Ex Post control.

"Ex Ante control" refers to the process of influencing the behavior of people to achieve organizational objectives before their behavior occurs. It is an attempt to motivate or cause people to strive to achieve organizational goals before the fact of their actual performance. "Ex Post control" refers to the process of influencing the behavior of people to achieve organizational goals after behavior has occurred. It is an attempt to influence a future set of actions by either reinforcing, failing to reinforce, or punishing behavior or performance which has already occurred. The notion of Ex Ante control is to influence the person's perceptions that his (her) effort will lead to outcomes (evaluations) which will be instrumental for attaining other desired outcomes (rewards). This suggests, in turn, that evaluation is inextricably related to reward systems, as examined in the next chapter.

Definition of Evaluation System

Evaluation is a ubiquitous process. It is a process which occurs, either formally or informally, in virtually all organizations. The evaluations derived may be valid or spurious; they be objective or biased - but they are ever-present in formal organizations. We may think of evaluation as the process of assessing or evaluating the present and potential contributions of people as organizational members. Stated differently, evaluation refers to the process through which an organization determines the value or worth of its human resources.

As typically observed in organizations, the evaluation process is variously termed "performance appraisal," "performance evaluation," and/or "promotability assessment." However, the key dimension that underlies actual systems of evaluation in organizations is the intent to determine one or more aspects of an individual's value to the firm.

Given this background, an "evaluation system" may be defined as a set of methods and processes designed to assess either some dimension of a person's contribution (present or potential) to an organization or the value of an individual as a whole to the firm. The evaluation system may isolate a particular dimension such as individual's productivity or promotability, as is typically done in practice; or, it may attempt to make an overall assessment of an individual's value to the firm. It should be noted that the former approach has been the traditional practice of evaluation, while the latter is the basis of the more recently developed field in Human Resource Accounting.[54]

Strategic Use of Evaluation in Control

The evaluation component of an overall control system can be used strategically to focus people's attention an the areas and things which are most critical for the organization to accomplish. The key to this is to incorporate the Key Result Areas from the corporate or subunit planning process into the evaluation system. This means that the performance areas which are the focus of evaluation must be the same areas included in the organizational plan.

The planning process generates the Mission, Key Result Areas, Objectives, and Goals which the organization seeks to attain. These must be the content which is in the performance evaluation process.

By focusing upon certain things and de-emphasizing others, organizations can use the evaluation process strategically to motivate people in desired directions. This specific mechanism by which this is accomplished involves the use of Key Result Areas (KRAs) in developing methods of evaluation.

METHODS OF EVALUATION

This section deals with the methods which may be used in evaluation. There are two fundamental issues in selecting an evaluation method: (1) the source of the evaluation, and (2) the technique or procedure by which the evaluation will be obtained.

Before examining these issues, we should consider the criteria to use to determine the extent to which a method of evaluation is appropriate. Our culture is heavily influenced by the value of "rationality." This, in turn, leads to a desire for objectivity in decision-making. In order to achieve objectivity in decisions, presumably we need objective information, including objective measurements. Thus, the ideal of an evaluation method would be to have objective (i.e., independently verifiable) measurements of performance or potential. Unfortunately, however, almost all methods of evaluation presently devised are based upon human judgment. As a result, they are inherently subjective. This must be recognized in considering the methods described below.

SOURCE OF EVALUATIONS

There are two basic types of evaluations: 1) judgmental sources, and 2) organizational measurements. Judgmental sources are the most commonly used. Basically, it involves obtaining judgments of performance or potential from various people. Another source is organizational measurements such as productivity or accounting measurements.

There are strengths and limitations involved with using either judgments or organizational measurements as sources. In principle, organizational measurements are objective. However, they may not take into account all significant factors of a person's performance and, therefore, may not be a valid index of performance. In addition, since people tend to pay greater attention to aspects of performance which are measured at the expense of aspects which are unmeasured, the use of measurements may lead to unintended dysfunctional results. For example, if a CPA firm uses chargeable hours (an organizational measurement) as the criterion for performance evaluation, then senior auditors may devote their efforts to maximizing chargeable hours at the expense of developing their subordinates. Similarly, if a plant manager is evaluated on the criterion of manufacturing efficiency rather than the unmeasured criterion of willingness to satisfy unusual customer demands, then efforts will be made to maximize efficiency even at the expense of dissatisfying present or potential customers.

Managers recognize that all important factors cannot be reduced to measurements. Thus more subjective judgmental methods are commonly used. However, these methods are certainly not free from difficulties. Judgments may be biased either for or against a person, consciously or unconsciously. Another problem of judgmental methods is the "halo effect," a tendency to generalize from one aspect of a person's performance to other aspects. For example, if a foreman is typically late in meeting production schedules, the plant manager may have a generally unfavorable impression of the foreman. He may generalize and evaluate the individual as being relatively poor in training his machine operators, inadequate in handling labor relations, and unsatisfactory in machine maintenance as well as simply tardy in meeting schedules. In this case, the overall bad impression has left a negative halo on the foreman.

Judgmental Evaluations

There are five basic sources of judgmental evaluation: 1) supervisors, 2) peers, 3) subordinates, 4) the person himself (herself), and 5) psychologists or assessment centers. They are each described in turn.

Supervisory Evaluations. This is the most common source of evaluations, although it is not necessarily a reliable source. A person's immediate supervisor is presumed to be in the "best" position to make evaluations because of knowledge derived from the supervisory process. However, either the halo effect or bias by lead to invalid evaluations.

For these reasons, it may be useful to use multiple rather than single assessments. For example, in CPA firms evaluations of performance are typically made after each "job" is completed. During the course of a year, a person is typically evaluated several times by different supervisors. Although the rating of a single supervisor may not be valid, the overall pattern of ratings provide an indication of performance and potential. The use of multiple ratings also enable the organization to interpret the ratings of evaluators who are known to be typically "difficult to please" or "easy."

Some firms use groups rather than merely a number of individuals to obtain evaluations. The appraisal group may consist of a person's immediate supervisor as well as other managers who have interacted with the individual. In some instances, there may be an evaluation committee which will include people who do not have a great deal of firsthand knowledge of people being evaluated. Their presence represents a trade-off between objectivity and actual knowledge of performance and potential.

Multiple ratings are, however, not free from limitations. It is possible that a person will acquire a "reputation" relatively early in his or her career. This may lead to the person being highly sought after, which, in turn, tends to lead to good assignments. This means that a person who makes a good first impression may continue to do so because of future assignments. This is known as a "self-fulfilling prophecy." Similarly, a person who does poorly at a relatively early stage may find himself (herself) the victim of a negative self-fulfilling prophecy.

Peer and Subordinate Evaluations. In order to overcome some of the undesirable aspects of supervisory evaluations and obtain another source of information about people, peer and subordinate evaluations are sometimes used. Peer evaluations developed out of "buddy rating" experiments conducted by the U.S. Military services during World War II.

Although these sources have attractive aspects, they are also not free from defects. One problem is that when peers rate each other there is the possibility for intentionally biased evaluations. Good friends may give each other mutually high ratings. In addition, if promotion and compensation decisions are based upon such ratings, a certain degree of "gamesmanship" may affect the evaluations provided. At times, the people being rated may prefer supervisory to peer evaluations, which can lead to resistance against the system.

The use of either supervisory or peer evaluations is sometimes of considerable practical importance in promotion decisions. Many union contracts state that jobs covered by contract are to be governed by seniority only when ability, skill and job performance are equal. This suggests that techniques for determining workers' potential for advancement must be acceptable to both unions and management. Unions may either prefer or not accept either one of these sources or the other in a particular instance.

Self Evaluations. Another source of evaluations are self-appraisals. Startling as the idea may seem, many organizations have experimented and support the use of self-evaluations. Typically, it is used as a supplement to the use of supervisory ratings.

Organizational Measurements

There is also a different type of source of information for evaluation. These are measurements which are routinely collected as part of the organizational management information system. They include accounting, production, marketing and related measurements. For example, the ratio of actual manufacturing cost to standard cost is that is generated from the accounting system might be used to evaluate a foreman and plant managers.

To illustrate the use of such measurements, consider the case of a manufacturer of paperboard boxes. Plants for manufacturing paperboard boxes are generally located near their markets and sources of supply in order to minimize or optimize transportation costs. This means that an organization may have several relatively small plants distributed throughout the country rather than a few large plants. As a result, plants tend to be comparable in terms of scale of operations. In this type of company, accounting and production measurements may typically be used to compare the efficiency and contribution to profit may be used as evaluation criteria.

It should be noted that there are difficulties involved in using such measurements for evaluation purposes. Differences in external factors such as unreliable sales forecasts may lead to manufacturing inefficiencies that are not controllable by foremen or plant managers, and yet influence the measurements by which they are evaluated. The age of machinery may differ from one plant to another and cause differences in productivity which are also uncontrollable. If a firm simply ranks plants and their managers using measurements of production efficiency, it may be a spurious representation of actual productivity. Thus, judgement is typically required in interpreting such measurements.

Another limitation of organizational measurements as evaluation criteria is the difficulty of using them in some industries. In large scale, continuous process industries such as oil production and refining, decisions about production tend to be centralized. Consequently, costly production changes may be scheduled for and beyond the control of operating management.

There are also many facets of performance which are important but not reflected in organizational measurements. In an automotive dealership, for example, the number of new and used cars sold and the dollar-value of parts are easily measured, but not the development of mechanics or customer relations. Similarly, in an optical products manufacturing company, production schedules may be achieved while labor relations deteriorate.

MEASUREMENT ASPECTS OF EVALUATION METHODS

We have examined the various sources of evaluations. Another important aspect of the evaluation process concerns the development of evaluation methods per se. Evaluations, as noted previously, are essentially nonmonetary measurements. In order to understand the different types of evaluation methods, it is necessary to first examine some fundamental aspects of measurement. For these aspects of measurement underlie the differences between various approaches to evaluation.

Measurement Defined

In chapter four, we noted that measurement is the process of assigning numerals to objects according to rules.[55] The different types of rules used to assign numerals to objects determines the scale or level of measurement which is achieved.

There are four basic scales or levels of measurement: 1) nominal, 2) ordinal, 3) interval, and 4) ratio.[56] Each of these scales is discussed below.

Nominal Scale. The nominal scale is the most basic level of measurement. The numbers assigned to objects in this scale do not have true significance; rather, they are merely numerical labels which are intended for purposes of classification.

A common example of the use of numbers as nominal measurement is in athletics. In football numbers used to identify players are also used to classify them. For example, all quarterbacks may be given numbers ranging from 10-19, while linemen may have numbers ranging from 70-99. Of course, there are exceptions: an offensive lineman may have the number 00.   Similarly, we could use numerals at the nominal measurement level to classify people according to their sex. If we identify or label women by the number 1 and men by the number 2, each person in class 1 is a woman and each in class 2 is a man. In this case, the numbers serve merely as a label to facilitate measurement by counting members of each category.

Ordinal Scale. The ordinal scale is the next higher level of measurement. The numbers assigned according to the rules of ordinal measurement do have arithmetic significance. The signify rank order.

The numbers assigned to indicate rank order may either be in ascending or descending direction. For example, 1, 2, . . ., n, can represent the highest, next highest, and so on to the smallest rank. Alternatively, it can represent the smallest, next smallest, and so on to the nth or highest rank.

A common example of measurement used to determine rank order is the "Compusport" method of evaluating football teams. This is a computer programmed method of evaluation. It assigns scores to various teams based on a variety of factors. If team A receives a score of 900 while team B receives a score of 800, the difference of 100 units is not necessarily empirically meaningful. All we can actually say is that team A ranks higher than team B.

Interval Scale. The interval scale is the next highest level of measurement. The numerals assigned according to rules of interval measurement have quantitative significance in the ordinary sense of the term. Thus the difference between a score of 8 assigned to person A and 10 assigned to person B is intended to represent the same thing as the difference between a score of 4 assigned to person C and 6 assigned to person D. The scale is intended, in other words, to represent an interval scale or level of measurement.

The interval scale represents different "distances" between objects in terms of numerical differences. Thus equal distances between objects are assigned equal numerals. For example, the difference between A and B's performance is 2 units (10-

8). The difference between C and D's performance is also 2 units.

Ratio Scale. The ratio scale is the highest level of measurement that can be achieved. The numerals assigned according to the rules of ratio measurement indicate the actual amounts or magnitude of the property being measured. The ratio scale has an empirical meaningful zero. This means that if an object has none of a property being measured, it will be assigned the number "zero." In addition, differences between objects are measured in equivalent units as different points on the scale. This is the same property as in interval scales.

Because the ratio scale has an empirically meaningful zero point, it can express the ratio between objects. Accordingly, if one object has twice as much of a property as another object, it is assigned a number twice as large.

EVALUATION METHODS

Although there are many different techniques of evaluation, they basically can be classified into three types: 1) rating methods, 2) comparison methods, and 3) descriptive methods. The various techniques which are included in each of these three categories are shown in Table 5-1.

These three categories of methods correspond very closely to three different scales or levels of measurement. Rating methods are, or purport to be, interval measures. Comparison methods are ordinal or rank order measures. Descriptive methods are essentially nominal measures. Table 5-1 also indicates the level of measurement achieved by each of the various techniques. The measurement aspects of these methods are discussed further below.

Rating Methods

"Rating methods" of evaluation involve the assignment of numerals to represent either 1) a person's performance or potential as whole or 2) specific dimensions or aspects of performance or potential. Essentially, then, it is a process of measuring performance, potential or components of these elements of a person's value in nonmonetary but quantitative terms.

Typically, rating methods focus not only upon an overall measure of performance or potential but upon their specific dimensions. Some of the aspects of performance commonly rated are: knowledge of job; personal qualities such as social skills, "dependability;" quantity of work; and quality of work. Some of the dimensions of potential commonly rated are leadership potential, initiative, and judgment.

Table 5-1 Evaluation Methods and Level of Measurement Achieved

NO.	EVALUATION METHOD		SCALE OF MEASUREMENT
I.	Rating Methods		
	A.	Graphic Rating Scale	Interval
II.	Comparison Methods		
	A.	Simple Ranking	Ordinal
	B.	Alternation Ranking	Ordinal
	C.	Paired Comparisons	Ordinal
	D.	Sociometric	Ordinal/Interval
	E.	Forced Distribution	Ordinal/Interval
III.	Descriptive Methods		
	A.	Checklists	Nominal
	B.	Essay	Nominal
	C.	Critical Incidents	Nominal
	D.	Evaluation by Objectives	Nominal

The rating approach may be used in various formats. However, the basic characteristic of all variations is that a set of attributes of a person are to be rated according to a standardized scale. The number and type of attributes or characteristics may vary. In addition, the set of numbers used in particular scales may vary form other scales. However, for a given scale they are designed to differentiate the extent to which group of people possess specified attributes.

Typically, some version of the "graphic rating scale" is used. For this technique, the evaluator is presented with a graph or chart listing performance characteristics. He (she) is asked to rate a person on these dimensions by placing a mark (a circle or check) on a scale provided. The scale may be descriptive or numerical. One type of descriptive scale uses words to rate performance such as: "always demonstrates good judgment" to "always demonstrates poor judgment." Another descriptive scale uses words such as "outstanding," "good," "satisfactory," "fair," and "poor." These descriptive ratings are then assigned numbers in order to convert them into scores. The verbal descriptions used are intended to represent equal distances or performance intervals. At a minimum, they are intended to represent "equal-appearing" intervals. This is necessary to score the descriptive rating and use it in comparing individuals. The rating scale used may also be numerical, which, by definition, does not require scoring. The evaluator is presented a range of numbers to use in rating a person on a set of dimensions. He (she) is instructed, for example, that "10" represents "exceptional performance" while "1" represents "extremely poor performance."

Figures 5-1 and 5-2 illustrate two rating forms which are used in a CPA firm. Figure 5-1 is a form used by supervisors to evaluate their subordinates, while Figure 5-2 is used by the subordinates to evaluate their supervisors. These forms are examples of the chart-type of rating approach.

Rating methods are commonly used in organizations. Their primary advantages are that they are relatively easy to use as compared with other methods, that they tend to have face-validity (they seem reasonable), and that they are relatively inexpensive to use.

Comparison Methods

"Comparison methods" of evaluation involve the ranking of people according to either 1) their overall job performance, potential or value to an organization or 2) specific dimensions of their value. People may be ranked on either a single criterion or a set of criteria.

The basic idea underlying the comparison method is that it is relatively "easier" for an evaluator to rank people to the extent to which they possess a given characteristic than to assign numerals to differentiate them. This means that the rankings derived are thought to possess a greater degree of validity than the rating measurements. The technical reason is that interval measurements (which rating scales purport to be) are more difficult to achieve than ordinal measurements (ranking).

There are several methods of deriving rankings: 1) simple ranking, 2) alternation ranking, 3) paired comparisons, 4) sociometric rankings, and 5) forced distributions.

Simple Ranking. Under this method evaluators are merely asked to rank employees from highest to lowest on some criterion or set of criteria. There are not instructions as to how this ranking should be derived.

Alternation Ranking. This method is a procedure designed to simplify the judgmental process involved in ranking, and, in turn, increase its reliability. Under this method, the person with the highest value on a criterion is selected first and ranked highest. Then the person with the lowest value on the criterion is selected. From the remaining

Figure 5-1
Audit Staff Evaluation Form

Name of Staff Accountant:		Classification:	Months With Company:		Age:
Name of Client:			Rate By:		
Name and Extent of Responsibilities:					
Length of Assignment:		Number Supervised:			
(Read Instructions Before Rating)			CHECK APPLICABLE BOX		
1.	Efficient Administration of Assignment				
	a. Proper planning of assignment.				
	b. Resourcefulness in the development of audit program.				
	c. Relating scope of work to internal control				
	d. Advising superiors immediately of reasons for increases in time requirements				
	e. Utilization of client personnel				
	f. Efficient use of staff men				
	g. Effective on-the-job training of assistants				
	h. Gaining respect of associates				
	i. Imagination in the development of points for management letters				
	j. Detection of the need of our auxiliary services for client development				
	k. Meeting of scheduled deadline dates				
	l. Effective completion of assignment within time allotted				
2.	Working paper evidence				
	a. Documentation of work performed, including adequate cross referencing				
	b. Conciseness with due regard to clearness of expression				
	c. Practical solutions to problems				
	d. Elimination of nonessentials				
	e. Sound conclusions and explanations				
	f. Completeness				
	g. Careful preparation				
	h. Legible handwriting				
	i. Accuracy				
3.	Technical ability				
	a. Adherence to generally accepted accounting principles				
	b. Auditing knowledge and application				
	c. Understanding S.E.C. regulations				
	d. Understanding federal and state income Taxes				
	e. Statement preparation				

Instructions

A careful, honest, and impartial preparation of this form is a must. Staff accountants are to be rated according to the standards of their present experience level.

This form should be completed before any assignment, *including preliminary work*, if it extends for *one week* or more.

Clarifying comments and recommendations *must be inserted in the space provided on the reverse side* for qualifications requiring improvement.

Only the PERFORMANCE QUALIFICATIONS above must be discussed with the staff accountant. Compliment on work well done and be constructive in your suggestions in areas where improvement is required.

DO NOT discuss the items on the reverse side with the staff accountant under any circumstances.

After the completion of this form and the discussion of the items above with the staff accountant, forward this form to the partner in charge of personnel in your office.

Figure 5-2
Supervisory Evaluation Form

Supervisor:		Assistant:			
Name of Client:			Rate By:		
Reviewed by:		Date:			
Length of Assignment:		Number Supervised:			
(Read Instructions Before Rating)		CHECK APPLICABLE BOX			
1. Planning					
a.	Presentation of a general overview of client's business				
b.	Presentation and discussion of prior year's workpapers				
c.	Conciseness and completeness of audit program				
d.	Definition of areas of responsibility				
e.	Explanation of time budget				
f.	Delegation of responsibility (to provide a challenging learning experience)				
2. Field Work					
a.	Introduction to client personnel				
b.	Introduction to client's records and procedures				
c.	Availability of supervisor				
d.	Willingness of supervisor to accept questions				
e.	Ability to communicate				
f.	Attentiveness to assistant's problems and needs				
g.	Allowed freedom of action				
3. Review					
a.	Promptness in reviewing assistant's work				
b.	Promptness in feedback to assistant				
c.	Ability to communicate queries on assistant's work				
d.	Instructional attitude toward the review process				
4. Evaluation					
a.	Promptness in evaluating assistant's work				
b.	Objectivity in evaluating assistant's work				
c.	Instructional attitude toward the evaluation process				
5. Professional Qualifications					
1.	Inquisitiveness				
2.	Creativeness				
3.	Aptitude for associating with people				
4.	Maintaining client relationships				
5.	Comprehension and interest in business of client				
6.	Interest in professional advancement				
7.	Advising superiors promptly of problems				
8.	Willingness to accept responsibility				
9.	Ability to accept responsibility				
10.	Ability to follow instructions				
11.	Effectiveness of expression - Oral				
12.	Effectiveness of expression - Written				

Figure 5-2 (cont'd.)

6.	Personal Qualifications				
1.	Appearance				
2.	Poise				
3.	Tact				
4.	Personality				
5.	Conduct				
6.	Cooperation -- Appreciation of mutuality of interests -- personal and company				
7.	Energy				
8.	Stability				
9.	Initiative				
10.	Decisiveness				
11.	Judgement				
12.	Maturity				
13.	Leadership				
14.	Integrity				
15.	Attitude				
16.	Desirable self-confidence				
17.	Attitude toward client & firm				
Explanations					

A. If I were to personally advise the supervisor on the areas in which he/she needs improvement, I would tell him/her..._____

_____

_____

B. I would *[ask for] [accept] [prefer not]* a future assignment with this supervisor.

C. **Comments** (Complete each sentence by circling the preferred response below)

1. The staff member *[is] [in not]* now qualified for heavier responsibilities (this does not necessarily relate to promotion).
2. I would *[ask for] [accept] [prefer not to have]* this staff member in my engagement hereafter.
3. In relation to this staff member's experience, the work assignment was *[complex] [moderately difficult] [relatively easy]*.
4. I *[have] [have not]* discussed this evaluation with the staff member.
5. The staff member's reaction to the discussion was *[receptive] [indifferent] [antagonistic]*.

Prepared by:	_____	**Date:**	_____
Discussed by:	_____	**Date:**	_____
Approved by:	_____	**Date:**	_____

Instructions

A thoughtful, unbiased preparation of this form is essential. This evaluation will serve as a means of obtaining information to be used in the development of supervisory skills.

This form should be completed for any assignment that extends for one week or more. It may be completed for assignments of shorter duration at the discretion of the staff assistant.

Upon completion, this form is to be forwarded to the personnel partner. The assistant should not discuss the evaluation with the supervisor.

people, the person with the highest value is selected followed by the person with the lowest value, and so on alternating between the next highest and lowest. Research on the reliability of this method has found it more reliable than the simple ranking method. An illustrative alternation ranking worksheet used at an insurance company is shown in Table 5-2. Its instructions are shown in Appendix 5-1.

Paired Comparisons. This is a method for deriving a ranking of people from a series of comparisons of each individual with all other people in the group to be ranked. A rank order may be derived from the paired comparisons by a simple scoring procedure. This method becomes cumbersome when the number of people to be ranked exceeds ten, because of the large number of pairs involved. It is typically implemented by writing the names of pairs of individuals on file cards and presenting them to evaluators one card at a time. Research on the reliability of the paired comparisons method has found it more reliable than simple ranking and equally reliable to the alternation ranking method.

Sociometric Ratings. This method is one that may be used with peers as the source of evaluations. It is based upon group choice. One person is asked to choose one or more other persons according to some criteria. The evaluators can be asked to use rating scales to assess others. They can also be asked to rank others on criteria. If the number to be ranked becomes too large, the method becomes quite cumbersome.

Forced Distribution. This method of forced comparison combines aspects of ratings as well as comparison methods. It requires the evaluator to distribute ratings to conform to a predetermined frequency distribution, typically a "normal distribution." For example, the evaluation must allocate 10% to the highest category in the scale, 20% to the next highest category, 40% of the middle of the scale, 20% in the next lowest category, and 10% in the lowest class in the scale. The method is analogous to "grading on a curve" in school situations.

The purpose of the forced distribution is to overcome any tendency for evaluators to either be too lenient or too severe in their ratings. However, the technique leads to an invalid assessment unless a group of individuals actually comprise a normal distribution in performance or potential.

Descriptive Methods

"Descriptive methods" of evaluation include a variety of procedures which are not designed to generate numerical evaluations, but, rather, are intended to describe or classify performance or potential. As the name implies, they are essentially descriptions of a person in terms of some criteria.

There are several different types of descriptive methods, including: 1) checklists, 2) essays, 3) critical incident technique, and 4) evaluation by objectives.

Table 5-2 Alternation Ranking Report - Claims

Worksheet for Appraising Relative Worth of Individuals

Employees to be Ranked		Ranking		Value in Current and Future Position Over the Next Five Years	
Number	Name	Number	Ranks	Ignoring Turnover	Considering Turnover
1	K.J.	1	HIGHEST		
2	K.R.	2	NEXT HIGHEST		
3	R.J.	3	NEXT HIGHEST		
4	S.J	4	NEXT HIGHEST		
5	M.G.	5	NEXT HIGHEST		
6	S.D.	6	NEXT HIGHEST		
7	B.L.	7	NEXT HIGHEST		
8	J.L.	8	NEXT HIGHEST		
9	O.A.	9	NEXT HIGHEST		
10	M.W.	10	NEXT HIGHEST		
11	M.J.	11	NEXT LOWEST		
12	S.W.	12	NEXT LOWEST		
13	J.V.	13	NEXT LOWEST		
14	B.L.	14	NEXT LOWEST		
15	K.F	15	NEXT LOWEST		
16	V.G.	16	LOWEST		

Checklists. The checklist is essentially a series of sets of statements that describe various types of behavior for a particular job. The behaviors described are specific aspects of effective and ineffective performance. The evaluator is required to "check" those statements which either most closely or least closely describe the behavior of a person.

The evaluator is presented both with sets of favorable and unfavorable items. The statements in each set are intended to <u>appear</u> approximately equally favorable or unfavorable, but they actually differ in the degree to which they have been found to be predictors of effective or ineffective performance.

The purpose of checklists is to force evaluators to make descriptions rather than evaluations. The former are presumed to be factual while the latter are more subjective. A major disadvantage of checklists is that they are costly to develop. they are also difficult to use by supervisors in counseling personnel, for evaluators do not know which are the critical items. This latter problem has led, in turn, to resistance against their use.

Essay Evaluation. This method of evaluation involves the use of an essay to describe aspects of a person's performance. Typically, there is not a prescribed format. The evaluator may be asked to describe a person's "strengths" and "limitations," or it may be used without any guidelines.

The method is helpful in the development process, but it is not as useful as other methods in providing a basis for administering reward systems. For it does not provide a convenient basis for personnel comparisons.

The essay method may be used with virtually all sources of evaluation, including self-assessments. However, its successful use requires evaluators with reasonable skill in written communication. Another potential limitation is that the method may be costly because of the time required to prepare evaluations. This may also lead to resistance against its use by evaluators.

Critical Incidents. This method involves recording significant (or critical) incidents of positive or negative performance as a basis for evaluation. It is related to the essay method of evaluation, for it is intended to describe actual performance.

There are no guidelines or criteria for determining what constitutes a critical incident. What is left to the evaluator's judgment, although a list of categories of job requirements may be provided. For example, critical incidents may occur in customer relations for salesmen, planning and decision-making managers, and in technical problem solving for engineers.

This method is intended to provide an "objective" basis for performance evaluation.

However, the choice of incidents to record as critical is still subjective. Because the method focuses upon actually observed behavior, it can be useful in the development process. Unless the incidents relate to characteristics required for promotability, it may not be particularly useful in promotion decisions.

Evaluation by Objectives. This method of evaluation is an outgrowth of the notion of management by objectives. It is built into the overall management process as a link in the chain of planning-performance-evaluation-planning. Thus it is closely related to the core control model presented in Chapter 2.

The underlying concepts are that people prefer to be evaluated according to criteria which they perceive are realistic and standards which they perceive are reasonably attainable. Under this method, people participate in setting the goals and identifying the criteria which will be used to evaluate them. Some of the results or goals on which people will be evaluated may be measurable in quantitative terms (such as profit, expenses, sales, or production volume), while others may be assessed qualitatively (such as employee development, customer relations or a marketing plan).

The basic steps in this cycle of evaluation are: 1) the evaluator and evaluatee mutually decide upon the key objectives for the evaluatee; 2) they agree on the criteria or measurements to be used in evaluating the achievement of performance objectives; 3) after performance occurs, actual performance is assessed against planned performance; and 4) objectives and criteria are revised for the future. In brief, this is both a sequential and an interactive process.

This method of evaluation is intended to focus on actual performance rather than on traits or skills. It is intended to describe the key dimensions of a person's role in order to give a clear picture of the aspects which are most significant and which will be emphasized in assessing performance. It is intended to emphasize the utilization and the developmental aspects of evaluation as well as the basic for compensation-reward decisions.

PROBLEMS OF EVALUATION METHODS

Although the evaluation methods described above are useful, individually or collectively they have a variety of limitations. The basic problem of evaluation methods may be thought of as either problems of 1) validity or 2) reliability.

Problems of Validity

Evaluations are intended to assess the performance and potential of people as organizational resources. However, they may not be valid measures of what they are intended to assess because of a variety of biases or errors made by evaluators.

The most common biases or errors which influence evaluations are: 1) the "halo effect", 2) different standards used, 3) inflation of standards, 4) bias, 5) central tendency, and 6) primary or recency of date. These are discussed below.

The Halo Effect. The so-called "halo effect" is the tendency for an evaluator to base an assessment of all individual characteristics which are presumably independent of each other on an overall impression of a person. For example, an individual who is generally well regarded may be rated high on such unrelated characteristics as technical skill, imagination and reliability. Another person, who is less well regarded, may be evaluated low on all these dimension even though an "objective" assessment would show that the latter person was more reliable than the former. Thus the halo effect is a tendency to generalize from an overall positive or negative impression to a set of specific traits or characteristics.

In general, the halo effect appears applicable to almost any method of evaluation, because it influences an evaluator's perception of an individual. Given an overall impression, the evaluator may be "set" to perceive certain things and filter out others or to perceive behavior in ways which are colored by "the halo" a person has. Thus the halo effect may influence the numbers assigned under rating methods, the ranks assigned under comparison methods, and may even influence the descriptions used under descriptive methods.

Different Standards. Evaluations may also lack validity because of differences in standards. One evaluator may use different standards in assessing performance than another. Thus the evaluation of the same person by two different people may be quite different because of differences in their criteria or weights assigned to those criteria. In addition, the same evaluator may employ different standards in assessing an individual at different points in time. An important problem for the valid use of evaluations is to obtain a common understanding of what standards ought to be used in evaluations.

Another aspect of differences in standards is a systematic error by evaluators. Some evaluators are known to be extremely difficult to please while others are quite lenient. Thus some people may be overvalued and others undervalued simply because of the evaluators used. To deal with this problem the organization must have knowledge of these tendencies. Over time, evaluators tend to develop reputations, and their evaluations are subjectively process or "interpreted." However, in the short run, an evaluator with a systematic error in standards may go unnoticed and cause invalid personnel decisions to result. This problem can be overcome by using several evaluators and averaging their measurements. This problem would seem to be less difficult with descriptive methods than with rating on comparison methods.

Inflation of Standards. Another problem involving the validity of evaluations is the inflation of ratings which has a tendency to occur. In some organizations there is a gradual inflation of ratings over time.

Bias. A major cause of invalid evaluations in organizations is bias on the part of evaluators. The bias may occur for a variety of reasons ranging from racial, religious or other prejudices to interpersonal conflict. In addition, an evaluator may simply not like the person being evaluated.

It is extremely difficult to deal with bias in evaluations. The descriptive methods offer less overt chance to present biased evaluations, but bias can certainly influence descriptive methods as well.

Central Tendency. This is a tendency of evaluators to avoid using the extremes of rating scales. There is, in other words, a tendency for ratings to cluster in a range around the midpoint (center) of the scale. This problem occurs with rating methods, but is avoided by either comparative or descriptive methods.

Bias from Primacy or Recency of Data. It is well-recognized in psychology that first impressions have a lasting influence. First impressions are lasting because they influence the way people perceive all subsequent data about a person. Similarly, recent impressions of people are also likely to be bias evaluations. There is a tendency to forget or overlook more distant data, with the exception of first impressions. Thus primacy or recency data about an individual may have an inordinate influence on evaluations. the problem occurs with all evaluation methods, with the possible exceptions of the critical incident and evaluation by objectives methods.

Problems of Reliability

Evaluations may lack reliability as well as validity. This is primarily attributable to the use of inconsistent application of standards by an evaluator at different times.

OVERALL ASSESSMENT OF EVALUATION METHODS

Each of the evaluation methods described have strengths and limitations. They are each capable of fulfilling the functions of the evaluation process to different extents. This section evaluates the evaluation methods. It summarizes their strengths and limitations and examines the degree to which they fulfill various evaluation functions. It also indicates some administrative problems with evaluation methods.

Summary of Limitations

Table 5-3 summarizes the extent to which various evaluation methods are subject to problems of validity and reliability. Rating methods are subject to a high degree to virtually all limitations discussed. Yet they are the common evaluation methods used because of their relatively low cost of administration and the convenience with which they may be applied. Comparison methods are sensitive to different and inconsistent standards as well as bias, but not to the halo effect, inflation of standards or central tendency. Descriptive methods are subject to these limitations to varying degrees depending upon their particular methods. However, the critical incident and evaluation by objective methods are the least subject to these problems. Unfortunately, they are the most complex and costly to administer.

Table 5-3 Limitations of Evaluation Methods

Methods	Degree to Which Each Limitation is Applicable					
	Halo Effect	Different Standards	Inflation of Standards	Bias	Central Tendency	Inconsistent Application of Standards
I. Rating Methods						
A. Graphic Rating Scale	High	High	High	High	High	High
II. Comparison Methods						
A. Sample Ranking	Low	High	Low	High	Low	High
B. Alternation Ranking	Low	High	Low	High	Low	High
C. Paired Comparisons	Low	High	Low	High	Low	High
D. Sociometric	Low	High	Low	High	Low	High
E. Forced Distribution	Low	High	Low	High	Low	High
III. Descriptive Methods						
A. Checklists	High	High	High	High	Low	High
B. Essay	High	High	High	High	Low	High
C. Critical Incidents	Low	Low	Low	Moderate	Low	Low
D. Evaluation of Objectives	Low	Low	Low	Low	Low	Low

Administrative Problems of Evaluation Systems

In addition to the problems of evaluation methods per se, there are also difficulties involved in administering the evaluation process as a whole. Two of the major problems are union resistance to evaluations and individual resistance.

Union contracts may contain a variety of provisions concerning compensation, promotion and retention. Management, thus, is not typically free to base its decisions in these areas upon evaluations alone. For example, unions may require that seniority governs promotion and layoff decisions. It may indicate, in an extreme case, that seniority is the primary criterion where a person is at least minimally able to perform a role. Thus the use of evaluation systems in such areas may be greatly constrained.

Unions may also retain some degree of control over the evaluation methods and judgments. Some methods may not be acceptable to unions. In addition, some union contracts may require a review process for evaluations.

Individuals as well as unions may resist evaluations for a variety of reason. Where an evaluation process results in criticism, people may, quite understandably, react defensively. In addition, since some of the methods may be quite subjective, people may simply not accept evaluations as valid. In some instances at least, they may be correct.

Another major reason for the failure of people to accept evaluations is their role in compensation and promotion decisions. Evaluations may play a critical role in a person's career. Thus it is quite natural that people may feel threatened by evaluations. The only response to such feelings is to develop an evaluation system which people perceive as being realistic, valid and reliable.

EVALUATION SYSTEMS AS COMPONENTS OF CONTROL SYSTEMS

In previous sections of this chapter we have examined the nature, functions, types, and limitations of evaluation systems as independent operating systems. We must also consider the functioning of evaluation systems as integral components of an overall core control system -- as a part of a larger system.

Purpose

The function of the evaluation system as a part of an overall control system is to simultaneously:

1.   provide a mechanism for assessing the value of contributions of people as a basis for administering rewards (Ex Post Control), and

2.   provide a mechanism for signaling the critical goals of an organization and
        people in order to motivate their efforts toward those goals (Ex Ante Control).

The system serves as a critical link between the measurement and reward systems.

The evaluation component of an overall control system can be used strategically to
focus people's attention an the areas and things which are most critical for the
organization to accomplish. The key to this is to incorporate the Key Result Areas
from the corporate or subunit planning process into the evaluation system. This means
that the performance areas which are the focus of evaluation must be the same areas
included in the organizational plan.

The planning process generates the Mission, Key Result Areas, Objectives, and Goals
which the organization seeks to attain. These must be the content which is in the
performance evaluation process.

By focusing upon certain things and de-emphasizing others, organizations can use the
evaluation process strategically to motivate people in desired directions. This specific
mechanism by which this is accomplished involves the use of Key Result Areas
(KRAs) in developing methods of evaluation.

Difficulties of Evaluation Systems in Control

In addition to the kinds of measurement and administrative difficulties of evaluation
systems per se, there can be major problems involved in using evaluation systems as
components of a core control system. Those difficulties can be viewed in classes:

1.   difficulties of interpreting measurements,
2.   difficulties of adjusting for suboptimization concealed by "objective"
        measurements, and
3.   the failure of measurement systems to focus upon all relevant key result
        variables.

These problems shall be examined in turn.

Interpretations of Measurements. Although all equivalent numerical representations
purport to be equal, this may be an illusion. For example, even though two profit
centers in the same company each earn $10 million pre-tax, the effective value of those
same two contributions may differ considerably.

The key to understanding this apparent paradox is this: The effective or relative value
(as opposed to the nominal or absolute value) of a measurement depends upon the
organization's goals. If profit center "A" earned $10 million but was budgeted at $5
million, we may evaluate its performance as superior. However, if profit center "B"

earned $10 million but was budgeted at $15 million, we might evaluate its performance as inferior.

In brief, not all equal numerical measurements are equal in substance. Some are more (and some are less) equal than others.

Suboptimization Concealed by Measurements. An important problem related to the above, and possibly a special case, concerns the difficulties of evaluating performance where measurements give the illusion of good performance. In some instances measurements may accurately show that performance for the specified unit is optimal, but may not reveal that this has occurred at the expense of other organizational units or the firm as a whole. For example, a division of an integrated company may purchase a component part used in its manufacturing process from a competitor rather than from a sister division because of lower price. Yet while this may maximize the purchaser's profits, it may suboptimize corporate profits as a whole.

Incomplete Measurement of Key Variables. Another major evaluation problem concerns the difficulties of assessing performance when not all key result variables have been measured. A typical problem found in organizations is the measurement of only some key result variables.

A manufacturing plant may have goals of production volume, cost savings, product quality, and safety. Yet the measurement systems and hence the data inputs toe the evaluation's system may only focus upon production volume and cost savings. This situation can lead management to make decisions which appear to give good results in the short term but are actually harmful in the long run.

SUMMARY

This chapter deals with the evaluation process. Evaluation refers to the methods developed to evaluate the performance and potential of people as organizational resources. Most evaluation methods involve some form of numerical measurement. The overall purpose of evaluation is to provide an input to the process of measuring individual and organizational performance as a component of an overall control system.

There are two basic sources of evaluations: 1) judgmental and 2) organizational measurements. Both have strengths and limitations. There are five basic sources of judgmental evaluations: 1) supervisors, 2) peers, 3) subordinates, 4) self, and 5) psychologists or assessment centers.

There are three basic types of evaluation methods: 1) rating methods, 2) comparison methods, and 3) descriptive methods. These three categories correspond closely to different scales of measurement -- interval, ordinal and nominal, respectively. Each of these evaluation methods is more suited to some evaluation functions than to others. For example, ratings are quite useful in selection decision, while descriptive methods are most useful in development.

All types of evaluation methods are subject to a variety of limitations. The basic problems may be viewed as either problems of 1) validity or 2) reliability. The specific difficulties include: The "halo effect", different standards, inflation of standards, bias, central tendency, and primacy or recency of data. Each method of evaluation suffers from these limitations to a different degree. For example, rating scales are quite susceptible to the problem of central tendency, while comparison methods and descriptive methods are not.

In spite of any imperfections, evaluation is a critical component of an overall organizational control system. It provides the basis for administering organizational rewards, as described in the next chapter.

APPENDIX 5-1: INSTRUCTIONS FOR ALTERNATION RANKING REPORTS

Please read these instructions carefully before completing the attached form.

The alternation ranking report is intended to provide a rank order of individuals according to judgments of their worth to the organization.

Column 1 - Consider these individuals only with respect to their current positions. Select the individual on the list who you feel has the highest value to the organization at the present time. Write his name in the space provided in Column 1. From the remaining names select the person who you feel is lowest in value to the organization at this time. Alternately, continue selecting the next highest and next lowest names remaining on the list. Indicate ties by placing the tied individuals' names in same space in Column 1.

Column 2 - Now that you have completed Column 1, consider these same individuals again. This time consider them with respect to both their current positions and the future positions they might occupy over the next five years. Ignore the possibility of the men leaving the company. Select the individual who you feel has the highest potential value to the organization. From the remaining names select the person who you feel has the lowest potential value to the organization. Alternately, continue selecting the next highest and next lowest names remaining on the list. Indicate ties by placing the tied individuals' names in the same space in Column 2.

Column 3 - Now that you have completed Column 2, consider these same individuals again. This time consider them with respect to both their current positions and the future positions they might occupy over the next five years; but do not ignore the possibility of the men leaving the company. Select the individual who you feel has the highest potential value to the organization. From the remaining names select the person who you feel has the lowest potential value to the organization. Alternately, continue selecting the next highest and next lowest names remaining on the list. Indicate ties by placing the tied individuals' names in the same space in Column 3.

ENDNOTES

52. For an alternative concept of the economic approach to control, see Eisenhardt, K.M., "Control: Organizational and Economic Approaches," <u>Management Science</u>, 1985, Vol. 31, pp. 134-149.
53. Ouchi, W., "A Conceptual Framework for the Design of Organizational Control Mechanisms," <u>Management Science</u>, 1979, pp. 833-847.
54. Flamholtz, E., <u>Human Resource Accounting</u> (San Francisco, CA: Jossey-Bass Publishers, 1985).
55. Stevens, S.S., "On the Theory of Scales of Measurement," <u>Science</u>, 103, No. 2684 (June 9, 1946), p.677.
56. Ibid.

REFERENCES

Chatman, J.A., "Matching People and Organizations: Selection and Socialization in Public Accounting Firms", Administrative Sciences Quarterly, 1991, **36**, 459-475.

Cleveland, J.N., Murphy, K.R., and R.E. Williams, "Multiple Uses of Performance Appraisal: Prevalence and Correlates", Journal of Applied Psychology, 1989, **74**, 130-135.

Earley, P.C., Connolly, T., and G. Ekegren, "Goals, Strategy Development and Task Performance: Some Limits on the Efficacy of Goal Setting", Journal of Applied Psychology, 1989, **74**, 34-33.

Earley, P.C., Northcraft, G.B., Lee, C., and Liturchy, T.R., "Impact of Process and Outcome Feedback on the Relation of Goal Setting to Task Performance:, Academy of Management Journal, 1990, **33**,1, 87-105.

Eisenhardt, K.M., "Control: Organizational and Economic Approaches", Management Science, 1985, **31**, 134-149.

Flamholtz, E., Human Resource Accounting, San Francisco, CA: Jossey Bass Publishers, 1985.

Gerlinger, J.M. and Louis Hebert, "Measuring Performance in International Joint Ventures", Journal of International Business Studies, 1989, **22**, 2, pp. 248-263.

Hedge, J.W. and M.J. Kavanagh, " Improving the Accuracy of Performance Evaluations: Comparison of Three Methods of Performance Appraiser Training", Journal of Applied Psychology, 1988, **73**, 68-73.

Konrad, A.M. and J. Pfeffer, "Do You Get What You Deserve? Factors Affecting the Relationship Between Productivity and Pay", Administrative Sciences Quarterly, 1991, **35**, 258-280.

Lewin, D. and Mitchell, D.J.B, "Appraisal and Reward," Chapter 7 of Human Resource Management: An Economic Approach, PWS - Kent/Wadsworth, forthcoming.

Liden, R.C., Mitchell, T.R., and C.E. Summer, "Top Level Management Priorities in Different Stages of the Organizational Life Cycle," Academy of Management Journal, 1985, **28**, 291-308.

Luckett, P.F. and M.K. Hirst, "The Impact of Feedback on Inter-Rater Agreement Insight in Performance Evaluation Decisions", Accounting, Organizations and Society, 1989, **14**, 379-389.

Matsui, T., Kakuyama, T., and M.L Uy Onglato, "Effects of Goals and Feedback on Performance in Groups", Journal of Applied Psychology, 1987, **72**, 3, 407-415.

Ouchi, W.,"A Conceptual Framework for the Design of Organizational Control Mechanisms", Management Science, 1979, 833-847.

Russell, J.A., and D.I. Goode, "An Analysis of Managers' Reactions to Their Own Performance Appraisal Feedback," Journal of Applied Psychology,1988, **73**, pp. 68-73,

Schmidt, F.I., Hunter, J.E., Outerbridge, A.N. and S. Gaff, "Joint Relation of Experience and Ability with Job Performance: Test of Three Hypotheses", Journal of Applied Psychology, 1988, **73**, pp. 56-67.

Shoorman, F.D., "Escalation Bias in Performance Appraisals: An Unintended Consequence of Supervisor in Hiring Decisions", Journal of Applied Psychology,1988, **73**, pp. 46-57

Snell, Scott A., "Control Theory in Strategic Human Resource Management: The Mediating Effect of Administrative Information", The Academy of Management Journal, 1992, **35**, 2.

Stevens, S.S., "On the Theory of Scales of Measurement," Science, 103, No. 2684 (June 9, 1946), p. 677.

Zalesny, M.D., "Rater Confidence and Social Influence in Performance Appraisals", Journal of Applied Psychology, 1990, **75**, 3, 274-289.

6

THE ROLE OF REWARD SYSTEMS IN CONTROL

This chapter examines the nature of organizational reward systems and their role in the core control system. The chapter focuses upon four basic questions:

1. What are reward systems?
2. What are their function in the organizational control process?
3. What are the major types of reward systems?
4. What are some issues to be resolved in the design of reward systems?

NATURE OF REWARD SYSTEMS

An "organizational reward system" is a set of methods and procedures designed to administer things which are valued by organizational members (termed "rewards") in order to simultaneously: 1) motivate people to achieve goals (Ex Ante Control), and 2) reinforce past behavior (Ex Post Control).

The functioning of a reward system is vital to the process of controlling human behavior in organizations. It helps determine not only performance in relation to current goals, but also influences the likelihood of people joining and remaining in an organization as well as the extent to which effort is directed to developing the organization's future capabilities.

If properly designed, reward systems can lead to desirable behavior for a firm. If incorrectly designed or administered, reward systems can lead to the gradual deterioration of an organization if not its abrupt demise.

This section presents an overview of the concepts and ideas underlying reward systems. This will serve as a basis for understanding their functioning and role as a component of organizational control systems.

Concept of Rewards

The basic idea to bear in mind is that reward systems are intended to motivate certain kinds of behaviors and to reinforce their occurrence. This means that the outcomes provided by the reward system must be positively valued by the person; if they are not valued, then they are not rewards. The outcomes may either be the inherent result of the person's own behavior, such as a feeling of accomplishment, or external to the person, such as the receipt of an increase in salary or a promotion.

Rewards are Subjective. Something that is generally regarded as a reward by most people may or may not be perceived as such by a given person. For example, a promotion that entails move from city X to city Y may not be perceived as a reward by an individual.

Types of Rewards

There are various types of "rewards" offered to members by organizations. There are "psychic," "financial," "intrinsic," "extrinsic," "nonmonetary," "monetary," and "social rewards."

Financial (Monetary) Rewards. Rewards that fall into this category are the most common medium of organizational motivation an reinforcement. They include wages and salaries as well as other aspects of compensation (bonuses, benefits, etc.).

Psychic Rewards. The term "psychic rewards" refers to the psychological experience of satisfaction derived by people from a variety of organizational rewards -- nonmonetary as well as monetary. An individual may derive psychic rewards (satisfaction) from promotions, favorable performance evaluations, verbal recognition, organizational prerogatives (such as a "special" parking space, office, etc.), or other rewards. The magnitude of the psychic reward is not necessarily a linear relation to the dollar-value of the reward. For example, an individual may derive a certain amount of satisfaction from a $1,000 raise, but not necessarily find as much satisfaction (it may be either more or less) from a $2,000 increase at a different point in time.

Intrinsic Rewards. This term refers to desirable outcomes which are the inherent result of a person's own behavior, such as enjoyment of a task. For example, a research chemist may derive intrinsic satisfaction from the act of research per se, a nurse may derive satisfaction from helping people, or a chef may derive satisfaction from seeing (or tasting) his (her) creations.

Extrinsic Rewards. These are rewards provided not only by the person himself but by others. They may include external evidence of recognition of accomplishment such as promotions, performance evaluations, and salary increases.

Nonmonetary Rewards. The term "nonmonetary rewards" refers to any organizational reward that is not financial in nature, such as promotions, performance appraisals, prerogatives, prestige, etc.

Social Rewards. These are rewards not provided by the organization per se, but which accrue to an individual because of his (her) membership in a firm. For example, certain organizations have considerable prestige, and members may derive "reflected glory" or prestige by being associated with such firms.

This discussion of the different types of rewards suggests that rewards may either be intangible or tangible. They may be tangible rewards such as salary increases or promotions, or intangible such as the satisfaction a person experiences from a "positive" performance evaluation. It should noted that even intangible rewards such as performance evaluations may also be valued by individuals as evidence of future tangible rewards. Stated differently, a series of positive performance evaluations may be perceived as leading to a very tangible salary increase or to a promotion.

ROLE OF REWARDS AS A COMPONENT OF CONTROL SYSTEMS

The primary function of rewards as a component of the core control system is to energize and motivate people to perform behaviors which are directed towards achieving organizational objectives and goals. The rewards offered or promised are the incentive for people to commit the energy and effort required to achieve organizational objectives and goals. Thus, they provide the Ex Ante incentive for people.

Rewards also provide the Ex Post source of reinforcement for people. Once people have expended energy based upon the expectation that they will be rewarded, the actual distribution of the rewards serves to reinforce the same behavior in subsequent time periods.

In brief, rewards are the component of an organizational control system which activates or energizes people's behavior. The planning component designs the desired direction of the behavior. The measurement component provides information about that behavior and input to the performance evaluation process which, in turn, provides the basis for administration of rewards. However, the rewards themselves are what people actually seek in exchange for their behavior.

TYPES OF REWARD SYSTEMS

The next step in understanding the role of rewards as a component of control id to examine the types of reward systems. There are three basic types of reward systems used in organizations. Two of these provide tangible rewards while the third provides intangible rewards.

Tangible rewards are provided by both (1) the compensation-reward system, and (2) the promotion-reward system. Intangible rewards, such as recognition, and evidence of future tangible rewards are provided by the evaluation system.

The role of the evaluation system as a component of a control system was described in Chapter 5. In brief, evaluation directs (motivates) attention to the relevant performance criteria. It also provides feedback on performance as a basis for either reinforcing or modifying it. Evaluation provides intangible rewards of recognition which are highly valued in our achievement-oriented society. The remainder of this chapter will focus upon compensation and promotional systems as rewards.

Compensation as a Reward System

"How does compensation operate as a reward system?" Compensation is a "reward" because it has the ability to lead to satisfying states of affairs for people. It has the ability to satisfy human wants.

Assumptions Underlying the Use of Compensation

This section examines how compensation functions as a reward system. It identifies the basic assumptions about how compensation influences human behavior.

People are concerned about a variety of needs: physiological, safety, self-esteem, social, and self-actualization. Money is a potential means to the satisfaction of these needs in two different but related ways. First, it is a medium of exchange which may be used to purchase goods and services to satisfy physiological and safety needs. In addition, because of its ability to obtain goods and services, money also has a generalized symbolic value for people. Stated differently, money is not only valuable as a means to obtain goods and services per se, but also as a symbol of achievement or success.

In many societies, including our own, the symbolic value of money leads to psychic satisfactions for a person. This means that a person may use money as a generalized satisfier for esteem, social and, and self-actualization needs. A person may use money income as a measure of his (or her) self-worth. In addition, income often has the potential for people to satisfy social needs, through the prestige it affords.

Thus, money has utility for people to satisfy needs. Its utility is psychological (symbolic) as well as economic. As a result, money, or more accurately, the opportunity to obtain money, is a powerful incentive to human behavior. This suggests that compensation functions as a reward because of the utility of money.

Subjective Value of Compensation

The value of money and, in turn, compensation to a person is subjective. This means that different people may "value" the same amount of money differently, because the same number of dollars may have a different utility for them. The same person may also value a given quantity of money differently at different times.

The value of compensation to a person has individual, group, and organizational determinants. These are examined below.

Individual Determinants. Assuming ceteris paribus, the value of money to people tends to assume the shape of an inverted U-shaped curve, as shown in Figure 6-1. This means that when a person has small amounts of money, its utility is relatively high and increases proportionately with the amount to be received. With increasing amounts of money, the marginal utility tends to decrease, and successive amounts contribute proportionately less satisfaction. Assuming that there is some "cost" to the individual to obtain the money (such as effort), at some point, the marginal value of money will actually tend to decrease with increases in money.

This means that although money may serve as a reward, it cannot be used as the only reward. In addition, it cannot be expected to function as a reward at all stages of a person's career.

One important implication for the management of human resources of the subjective value of compensation is that the same increments of income will produce different motivational responses from different people and from the same people at different times. This means that compensation decisions for groups such as factory workers, engineers, and managers may have to take a variety of diverse factors into account. Similarly, even decisions for a specific group such as managers may have to take into account differences in the value of compensation. For example, young M.B.A.'s typically want high pay and are less concerned about security and retirement benefits, while older managers are more concerned about security and retirement than current income.

Group Determinants. In addition to these individual determinants of the subjective value of money, there are also other important influences. For example, an individual's social needs may outweigh his (her) need for money. In certain work situations, individuals may face conflicts between the need for acceptance and approval by management. The former provides social satisfactions while the latter provides compensation.

If a person fails to conform to group norms, then the result can be criticism, ridicule, or ostracism. Thus individuals must make decisions concerning the value of compensation and the cost (and probability) of social disapproval.

Organizational Determinants. The value of compensation to a person also depends upon the extent to which it is perceived as equitable or fair relative to the compensation of others in the same organization. If a person does not perceive compensation to be equitable, the result is tension and cognitive dissonance.

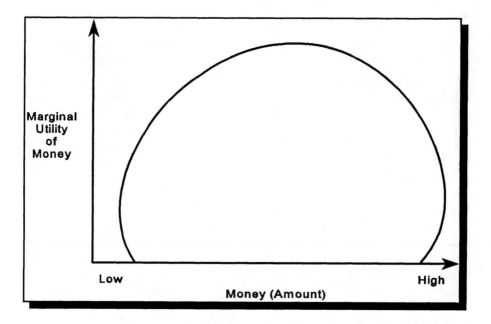

Figure 6-1
Hypothesized Subjective Value of Money

Several theories have been proposed which suggest that people seek a "just" or "equitable" return for their contributions of services on a job. The basic idea underlying such theories is that compensation which is either greater than or less than that which is perceived by the recipient to be equitable results in dissatisfaction. This is analogous to the oft-quoted union demand for "a fair day's pay for a fair day's work."

Summary

In brief, compensation has the power to serve as an important motivator of behavior because money is capable of satisfying human needs. Money has the ability to satisfy needs both because of its use to obtain goods and services and because of its generalized value as a symbol of the ability to obtain need satisfaction.

The value of money as a motivator for any person is subjective. It depends upon individual (personal), group, and organizational factors. Different people have a different utility for money, and its utility may also differ for the same person at different times.

STRATEGIC USE COMPENSATION AS REWARD

The previous section has explained why and how compensation serves as a reward. This section deals with the strategic use of compensation as a reward. more specifically, it suggests how to use compensation as a reward in a core control system.

First we shall examine the nature of compensation, per se, and then we will discuss the strategic use of compensation, per se.

Nature of Compensation

"Compensation" may be defined as the financial rewards paid to people for services rendered to an organization. Although it is typically paid in money, it may also be paid in the form of goods and services.

There are two basic forms of compensation, commonly known as "wages" and "salaries." The term "wages" refers to compensation paid on an hourly, daily, or piece-work basis. It is generally used for compensating manual labor. The term "salaries" refers to compensation paid for a period of a week, month, or longer duration. It is generally used to compensate clerical of managerial employees.

The difference between wages and salaries is related to the different functions of compensation. Some suggest that salaries are paid for services requiring special training or abilities. Yet a machine operator may be highly skilled and receive an hourly wage paid on a daily basis, while and office clerk may be relatively unskilled and receive a "salary." Similarly, a salesman may have considerable skill and be compensated by commission (a form of piece work), while someone of equivalent (or less) skill may receive a salary. Thus the rationale for using wages for one type of employee and salaries for another is not solely attributable to the variable of skill.

Type of Compensation in Relation to Work

A major factor explaining choice of wages or salaries depends upon the nature of the work performed and, in turn, the extent to which it is feasible to measure units of services rendered. For some jobs, such as certain factory workers, salesmen, or typists, it is possible to measure (i.e., count) the units of services (production) rendered. For others, such as managers or secretaries, it is virtually impossible to measure all aspects of work performed. Thus different modes of compensation have developed to deal with this difference.

The two basic modes of compensation are: 1) time-based compensation and 2) quantity-based compensation. The former involves payment for specified time periods: hour, day, week, month, year, etc. The latter involves payment for the units of service rendered (number of telephone calls made, rooms painted, circuits wired, etc.).

Compensation Strategy

The key principal underlying compensation ought to be, "form follows function." This means that the method of compensation and the elements of the compensation plan should be designed in such a way as to optimize the probability that people will behave in desired ways. Although this seems logical and, perhaps, even obvious, it id not found often enough in actual compensation systems. To implement this principal, compensation systems must be geared toward optimizing the performance of people on their own and the organization's Key Result Areas. This means that compensation should be directed to the MAXIMUM extent feasible toward people to be concerned about achieving the mission and goals developed in the plan of their strategic business unit. This is done by linking rewards to the achievement of the plan.

Some organizations have compensation systems which provide bonuses linked to performance against key result areas. In most cases, each Key Result Area receives a weight that determines the percentage of the bonus that can be earned by differing degrees of performance on the variable. For example, a plant manager may have several Key Result Areas, including; manufacturing efficiency, quality, scrap, and the like. Weights may be allocated to each KRA: Manufacturing (30%), Quality (30%),Scrap (5%), safety (10%), etc. It is through this process that compensation can be used strategically to incentivize people to focus upon certain areas.

PROMOTION-REWARD SYSTEMS

In the previous portion of this chapter we have described the nature and methods of the compensation-reward system. This section focuses upon another major element of the overall organizational reward system -- the promotion reward system.

It should be noted at the outset that neither theory nor practice is as well developed for the promotion-reward system as for the compensation or evaluation reward system. Unlike compensation decisions, promotion decisions typically occur as a by-product of the selection process to fill job vacancies. Consequently, many organizations do little or no formal planning of the promotion process; rather, it just happens. Just as practice in this area is not well developed, theory about promotion as a reward is rather sparse.

The purpose of this section is to outline the rationale for promotion as a reward. It also will describe some guidelines for using promotion-reward system as a component of a core control system.

Promotion as a Reward

How does a promotion operate as a reward? In other words, what makes a promotion attractive to people and motivates them to behave in ways which may help achieve it?

Although the term "promotion" has been defined in many different ways, it basically refers to a person's movement from one position level in a job hierarchy to another of higher rank. The increase in rank may be attributable to increases in skill, responsibility or even some artificial or illusory factor. For example, a promotion may consist of movement from the position of machinist to foreman, from salesman to sales manager, from vice president to president. These promotions may reflect real differences in function performed. However, there are also "nominal" promotions, which merely use job titles to reflect artificial distinctions between positions. For example, in one insurance company a promotion from claims investigator to claims adjuster did not reflect any real difference in function; rather, it merely reflected the amount of time a person was with the firm. Similarly, the titles assistant engineer, engineer, and senior engineer may reflect only artificial differences. They are used, as explained subsequently, to provide the _illusion_ of promotion because of its power as a motivator. There are also promotions which reflect differences in attainment and imply differences in skill rather than differences in function. In colleges and universities, for example, promotion from assistant to associate to full professor is intended to be a recognition of such achievement differences.

Ability to Satisfy Various Needs. The power of promotion as a reward is derived from its attractiveness to satisfy a variety of needs for an individual. Promotion per se has important symbolic value for people in our society. It represents an increase in status in one's organization, which, in turn, may confer social as well as organizational prestige. Promotion also represents "recognition," that is, formal acknowledgment by an organization of a person's increased value to the enterprise. Thus it is a vehicle for people to satisfy their self-esteem needs.

Promotion also has power to help satisfy self-actualization needs. The increase in rank may provide the opportunity for a person to exercise latent abilities, to assume higher levels of responsibility. It may provide, in other words, the opportunity for people to more fully become what they are capable of becoming.

In addition to its power in satisfying such higher level needs, promotion also indirectly enables a person to increase satisfaction of physiological and perhaps even safety needs. Typically, an increase in compensation accompanies a promotion -- at least it tends to correlate with genuine and not artificial promotions. This means that promotion not only has values of its own but also the values of compensation as a reward.

Subjective Value of Promotion. Just as compensation, the value of promotion is different for different people and for the same person at different times. Many people in our society are highly achievement-oriented. For them, promotion is a valued reward. For others, who may have a somewhat lower need for achievement and who value other variables such as security or social relations, a promotion may have less value or even a negative value (or cost).

There are a variety of reasons why people do not always value promotions. For example, a salesman in a automotive dealership may earn more than the sales manager. The latter may have greater job security, but this may be less important to the salesmen who values money per se. Indeed, this problem commonly plagues a variety of companies who find salesmen unreceptive to "promotions" to sales managers where they may actually earn less. A factory worker may not wish promotion to foreman because he will no longer be able to associate with his peers (that is, be "one of the boys"). In addition, he may be concerned about a loss of union protection, if foremen are not part of the bargaining unit, and loss of seniority rights, in case of layoff. An engineer who is highly oriented to the technical side of his job may not desire to be promoted to engineering manager because it will take him away from the work he truly enjoys. Another person may not wish a promotion because it involves a geographical change. As the number of two-career families (husband and wife) increases, such geographical changes become quite complex for people.

Use of Artificial Promotions. Since organizations are well-aware of the motivational power of promotion, some have even developed artificial job grade distinctions and/or inflated job titles to tap the desire of people for promotion. For example, the banking industry is well-known for its use of titles, such as Assistant Vice President, Vice President, Senior Vice President, to capture the psychic advantages of the vice presidential title. The use of the titles assistant engineer, engineer, and senior engineer is another example of somewhat artificial promotions.

Power as Long-Term Motivator. One of the great values of promotion as an organizational reward is that it has the ability to motivate long-term commitment and performance. Individuals may have some ultimate concept of the level they aspire to attain in the organizational hierarchy. In one of the giant manufacturing corporations such as General Motors, IBM, an individual may aspire to become a top executive, such as President, V.P.-Manufacturing or Controller. Alternately, the person may wish to become Plant Manager or District Sales Manager either as an end in itself or as a step in further advancement. Similarly, the possibility of becoming a partner in one of the large, international CPA firms, such as Price Waterhouse & Co., or Coopers and Lybrand motivates individuals for many years' effort.

This means that people are directing long-term energies on such career goals. Thus promotion is a complementary part of the overall organizational reward system. It is the ingredient for long-term motivation.

Design of Promotion-Reward Systems

We have examined the role of promotion-reward systems as a motivational tool. The next step is to consider how they may be designed to be effective. As noted above, it is unfortunate that our theory and practice of managing the promotion process is not presently well-developed. However, there are certain guidelines and issues which are outlined below.

Fundamentals of Promotions-Rewards System. There are four basic factors which must be considered in designing the promotion-reward system: (1) promotion policies, (2) promotion channels, (3) procedures for assessment and selection, and (4) the promotion decision-making process per se.

One of the primary factors involved in designing the promotion-reward system is policy. One of the major policy questions concerns the issue of whether a firm should hire people from outside the organization for higher level positions. Stated differently, what should be the highest entry-level position into the organization?

Organizations follow different strategies to this issue. Some, like IBM and DuPont, tend to hire only at relatively low-level entry positions and promote people from within to fill higher job level vacancies.[57] The rationale for this policy is that (1) it serves as a motivator to personnel who have the opportunity for promotion, and (2) it insures that people will be familiar with the organization and not just a particular type of function (i.e., controllership) when they occupy higher level jobs. Such organizations believe that it is often quite risky to hire from the outside to fill high-level positions. For example, several years ago one of the "Big 3" automotive manufacturers hired an Executive Vice President from one of its competitors to become its President. A few years later, that person left the firm. The problem was that it is difficult to "transplant" such an important "organ" as a chief executive from one body to another without the risk of "rejection." Of course, many other firms believe strongly in the virtues of hiring from the outside, and there have been many successful transplants. For example, some personnel executives in the banking industry believe that the officer-level position in their organizations are relatively homogeneous across most comparably-sized banks. Thus they may recruit for such positions from the outside. However, from the point of view of the promotion-reward system, a policy of internal recruitment is a powerful motivator.

Another major factor involved in the system's design is the identification of promotion channels. At an elementary level, the promotion channels may be identified by reference to an organization chart. However, the development of people may require promotion paths that do not correspond to movement from foreman to assistant plant manager to plant manager. Rather, it may involve movement from plant manager to assistant personnel director to some job title in sales in order to develop broad knowledge of a business.

A third element of the promotion-reward system is the methods and procedures used for assessment and selection of people. It is important to distinguish between the methods and procedures used for (1) unionized personnel and (2) nonunion personnel.

The promotion methods, procedures, and criteria for unionized employees may be relatively spelled out in collective bargaining agreements. Unions tend to want seniority as the primary, if not the sole, criterion for promotion decisions. It is an objective criterion, and seniority (length of service) is presumed to correlate with experience and skill. In addition, unions typically may file a grievance and submit a promotion decision to arbitration if they disagree with management's choice. For nonunionized personnel, promotion typically occurs as a by-product of the human resource planning, acquisition and allocation process.

The ultimate step in designing this system is the promotion decision-making process per se. This ranges from a very informal, almost casual process to a very structured, sometimes ritualized process. In some organizations a group of executives virtually decide promotion during luncheon conversations, while in others openings may be posted and "bids" (applications) requested.

The promotion decision is inevitably a subjective process. There are no machines to measure "promotability." Thus, it is possible for error as well as bias to creep into decisions.

Strategic Use of Promotions

Promotions are a valuable reward, and they can be used strategically as a component of a reward system. The key to the effective use of promotion as a strategic reward relates to the ability of promotions to send a "signal" or "message" throughout the organization.

The message sent by promotions concerns who is valued. People throughout organizations "analyze" promotions to determine why the people promoted were valued sufficiently highly to be promoted. They, in turn, may tend to model their own behavior on that of the promoted individual(s). This means that people who are promoted tend to become corporate role models. If, for example, a manager has a reputation of being a leader in quality improvement, and that manager is promoted, the message received by the organization is that, "quality is valid." On the contrary, if a plant manager has a high efficiency rating but is not known for either customer responsiveness or quality and that manager is promoted, a totally different message will be received. In the latter case, the message is that, "efficiency counts and customer responsiveness and quality do not."

It is this phenomenon of organizational messages being sent, or a least inferred, that facilitate the strategic use of promotional decisions. Management can influence the message sent by specific promotion decisions. If an organization wants to motivate people to behave in a strategic way, it must reward that behavior. A promotion is only one of the clearest signals that can be sent to an organization. On the contrary, if management says that they want one thing and reward people who behave inconsistently with what they say they want, they will be accused of: "Not walking the talk." This is what Kerr has referred to as: "The folly of rewarding A while hoping for B."[58]

Complementary Functions of Reward Systems

This chapter has described two major components of the overall human resource reward system: the compensation and promotion reward systems. Together with the evaluation system, these reward systems provide the mechanism by which organizations motivate and reinforce people toward joining, retaining membership, developing their skills, and performing their roles.

The three systems complement one another. They serve different types of functions and emphasize different time periods. Compensation plays a greater role in attracting human resources than promotion or evaluation (the latter is irrelevant at that point). Promotion and, perhaps to a lesser extent, compensation play major roles in helping to maintain people in the organization. Evaluation is the most immediate system influencing performance, but it is only instrumental for the individual who desires either compensation or promotion.

Evaluation is typically the reward system that can provide the most immediate feedback and reinforcement for people. Compensation may be used for both short-term and long-term motivation and reinforcement. Promotion tends to be a medium-term to long-term motivator.

The differential functions and time horizons of these systems suggest that they must be integrated into an "effective" overall reward system in a particular organization -- one that motivates behavior congruent with organizational goals and individual needs.

DIFFICULTIES OF REWARD SYSTEMS

An organizational reward system is a powerful task of motivation and control. A properly designed reward system can produce behavior designed to achieve organizational goals. However, a reward system is merely a tool and if it is not properly designed it can produced behavior which is contrary to an organizations interest.

A reward system will typically produce the behavior it has been <u>designed to produce,</u> <u>whether or not</u> these programmed results were the behaviors it was <u>intended to</u>

produce. Stated differently, to evaluate the effectiveness of a reward system, we must examine the behaviors the system actually encourages rather than merely the behavior it wad intended to encourage.

Another major problem with reward systems is that if they are not properly designed, they will lead to short-term thinking rather than a long-term orientation. This is a major difficulty with reward systems.

SUMMARY

This chapter has focused upon the reward system as a whole and the compensation and promotion reward subsystems. A reward system is a management control subsystem designed to motivate people toward the achievement of organizational goals. "Rewards" are the desirable outcomes or returns to a person, provided by himself and others. Rewards are subjective. Whether an "object" (tangible or intangible) is a reward is determined by a person's needs and perception. There are three major types of human resource reward systems: (1) evaluation, (2) compensation, and (3) promotion.

Compensation functions as a reward because it has the ability to lead to people's need satisfaction. It has the ability to satisfy needs not only as a medium of exchange to acquire goods and services but also for its symbolic values. It is viewed as evidence of achievement and worth to an organization and society. The value of compensation to an individual is subjective and has personal, group and organizational determinants.

There are two major forms of compensation: wages, which are based on hourly work and tend to be paid for manual labor, and salaries, which tend to be paid for periods of one week or longer and are generally used to compensate clerical or managerial personnel.

Promotion functions as a reward because it has the power to satisfy a variety of human needs. Promotion has considerable symbolic value in our society because it represents an increase in status. It represents recognition of an increase in a person's value to an enterprise. Since it is typically accompanied by an increase in compensation, it also has the power to help satisfy physiological and safety needs. Just as compensation, promotion has a subjective value. Because they recognize the power of promotion as a motivator in an achievement-oriented society, some organizations use "artificial promotions," that is, they create artificial job grade distinctions and/or inflated job titles. The theory and practice of promotion-reward systems is not yet well-developed. In many organizations the promotion process tends to occur as a by-product of the need to fill job vacancies. there are four basic aspects of the design of a promotion-reward system: (1) formulating promotion policies, (2) identifying promotion channels, (3) developing procedures for assessment and selection, and (4) the promotion decision per se. Because of the subjective nature of the promotion decision, great care must be exercised to insure that decisions are valid.

Both compensation and promotion can be used strategically as part of a control system. Compensation can be used to channel people's efforts toward the organization's overall mission and/or specific Key Result Areas, objectives, and goals. Promotion decisions send "messages" throughout the organization concerning who and what is valued. This, in turn, creates corporate role models. Management can use promotions to create the appropriate role models to strategically focus people on the things it values.

ENDNOTES

57. The appointment of Louis Gerstner, Jr. as IBM's Chairman in 1993 from RJR Nabisco is a notable exception, and may signal a change in future corporate practices in this regard.

58. Kerr, S. "On the Folly of Rewarding A, While Hoping for B," <u>Academy of Management Journal</u>, 1975, Vol. 18, pp. 769-783.

REFERENCES

Conlon, Edward.J. and Parks, J.M., "Effects of Monitoring and Tradition on Compensation Arrangements: An Experiment with Principal-Agent Dyads", Academy of Management Journal, 1990, 33, 603-633.

Cowherd, D.W. and D. I. Levine, "Product Quality and Pay Equity Between Lower-Level Employees and Top Management: An Investigation of Distributive Justice Theory", Administrative Sciences Quarterly, 1992, 37, 2, 302-321. Gerlinger, J.M. and L. Hebert, "Measuring Performance in International Joint Ventures", Journal of International Business Studies, 1991, 22, 249-263.

Gerhart, B., and G.I. Milkovitch, "Organizational Differences in Managerial Compensation and Financial Performance", Academy of Management Journal, 1990, 33, 663-691.

Gomez-Meija, L.R., Tosi, H., and T. Hinkin, "Managerial Control, Performance, and Executive Compensation, Academy of Management Journal, 1987, 30, 51-70.

Harder, J.W., "Play for Pay: Effects of Inequity in a Pay-For-Performance Context", Administrative Sciences Quarterly, 1992, 37, 2, 321-335.

Kerr, J.L., "Diversification Strategies and Managerial Rewards: An Empirical Study", Academy of Management Journal, 1985, 28, 155-169.

Kerr, S., "On the Folly of Rewarding A, While Hoping for B," Academy of Management Journal, 1975, Vol. 18, 769-783.

Konrad A.M. and J. Pfeffer, "Do You Get What You Deserve? Factors Affecting the Relationship Between Productivity and Pay", Administrative Sciences Quarterly, 1990, 35, 258-280.

Micelli, M.P., Jung, I., Near, J.P.M. and Greenberger, D.B., "Predictors and Outcomes of Reactions to Pay-For-Performance Plans", Journal of Applied Psychology, 1990, 75, 2, 508-521 .

Pierce, J.L. Stevenson. W.B., and James L. Perry, "Managerial Compensation Based on Organizational Performance: A Time Series Analysis of the Effects of Merit Pay", Academy of Management Journal, 1985, 28, 261-278.

Tosi, H.L. and Gomez-Meija, L., "The Decoupling of CEO Pay and Performance: An Agency Theory Perspective", Administrative Sciences Quarterly, 1989, 34, 2, 252-278.

Townsend, A.M., K.D. Scott, and S.E. Markham, "An Examination of Country and Culture-Based Differences in Compensation Practices", Journal of International Business Studies, 1990, 667-678.

Williams, M.L. and G.F. Dreher, "Compensation System Attributes and Applicant Pool Characteristics", Academy of Management Journal, 35, 1992.

Zenger, T.R., "Why Do Employers Only Reward Extreme Performance? Examining the Relationships Among Performance, Pay and Turnover", Administrative Sciences Quarterly, 1992, 37, 2, 198-219.

7

THE ROLE OF ORGANIZATIONAL STRUCTURE AND CULTURE IN CONTROL

The model of an organizational control system presented in Chapter 2 (Figure 2-1) included three parts: 1) the core control system[59], 2) organizational structure[60], and 3) organizational culture[61]. The components of the core control system have been examined in Chapters 3-6. This chapter deals with the role or organizational structure and culture in control. It also suggests the relationship between structure and culture and the core control systems.

ROLE OF ORGANIZATIONAL STRUCTURE IN CONTROL

As used in this context, the term "organizational structure" refers to the patterned relationships among the roles people occupy in a formal organization.[62] "Roles," in turn, are sets of behaviors expected to be performed by an incumbent.

Stated differently, roles refer to the jobs people occupy in organization, and to the sets of behavioral requirements expected to be performed by people in those jobs. An organization's structure refers to the pattern of arrangements of the sets of jobs comprising the organization. Thus there are two major elements of structure: 1) roles, and 2) their patterned arrangement in relation to one another.

The Control Functions of Structure

Organizational theorists as well as practicing managers have long recognized that an organization's structure performs important functions in influencing the behavior of people in an organization. Structure performs functions of control in two different but related ways: 1) through the mechanism of an organizational role per se, and 2) through the pattern of arrangements of roles.

Control Functions of a Role. By definition, a role specifies a set of expected behaviors. It prescribes the responsibilities of the person--any person--who occupies the role. These responsibilities are specified as Key Result Areas.

Through the process of specifying what Key Result Areas ought to be in a given role, the role itself serves as a "goal" or standard against which a person's actual behavior can be monitored (or measured), evaluated, and rewarded.

Roles can be explicit or implicit. In large, professionally managed organizations, roles are typically explicit in terms of job descriptions. In smaller, entrepreneurial firms, roles are not typically defined formally, but tend to be left implicit. The greater the degree to which a role is defined formally, the greater the degree of organizational control that is feasible.

Control Function of the Arrangement of Roles. The pattern by which roles are arranged in relation to one another also performs a control function. Roles can be arranged in a large variety of patterns and structures. The patterns can vary from relatively flat organizational hierarchies, as illustrated in Figure 7-1, to relatively tall structures, as shown in Figure 7-2.

Factors Influencing Structures of Roles

One factor that may lead to the choice of a flat or tall structure is simply the size of an organization. The greater the number of people involved, the greater the need for intermediate levels of management to achieve correlation and control. Management theory has developed notions such as "span of control" to refer to this aspect of organizational structure.

Effects of Size. As an organization increases in size from a relatively small entrepreneurship, such as the firm illustrated in Figure 7-1, the classic response is to develop functional specialization. Initially, the "president" is typically an owner-manager-player; that is, he or she typically does whatever is necessary to operate the firm. This may range from executive decisions involving capital budgeting expenditures to supervising sales and clerical persons, or to selling product to customers. However, as the business expands, specialists may be added to perform specific functions. For example, the firm may hire an accountant, a sales manager, or personnel manager. When these events occur, the organization's structure must inevitably shift to the tall-form of structure shown in Figure 7-2.

Centralization vs. Decentralization. In addition to the effect of size upon the organizational structure, another major factor is a strategic management decision concerning the degree of autonomy (or self control) people should be permitted in running the organization on a day to day basis: this decision is reflected in the degree to which the organization's structure is "centralized" or "decentralized".

Under a centralized organizational structure, most of the major decisions (operational as well as strategic) are made by corporate-level management rather than divisional or branch personnel. For example, in a centralized specialty retail manufacturer and distributor, decisions involving what goods to manufacture or purchase are made by corporate design and purchasing executive rather than by the firm's regional sales manager. In this firm, the latter's role involves administration of day to day operations

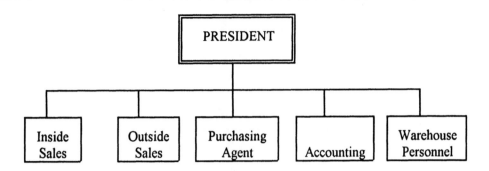

Figure 7-1
Illustration of Flat Organization Structure

(recruitment, training, sales, record keeping, and inventory control) rather than profit responsibility. The rationale is that there are corporate level experts who can best make decisions which are then implemented by lower level managers.

Under a decentralized organizational structure, an attempt is made to delegate as many decisions as possible to divisional or branch levels of responsibility, rather than making them at the corporate level. The rationale is that each divisional, departmental, or branch manager should be permitted, to the maximum extent feasible, to run his or her organizational unit as though it were their own business, subject only to corporate level periodic review. In a decentralized system of management, each business or organizational unit is evaluated prospectively (Ex Ante Control) and retrospectively (Ex Post Control) on financial and other criteria.

One of the factors affecting the choice of a centralized versus a decentralized management system is size. The larger an organization, the greater the difficulty of using a centralized system, because top management can become overwhelmed with detail or lose touch with many diverse operations. However, a decentralized system requires "strong" managers. This means managers who are capable of managing a business as if it were their own, and performing all of the basic managerial functions.

In brief, there are advantages as well as disadvantages to centralized and decentralized organizational structures. Similarly, in basketball or football there are advantages and disadvantages to zone defenses versus "man-to-man" defenses. A coach choosing one of these defenses gives up one thing to get something else. For example, without a seven-foot center a coach may choose a zone defense to get an advantage in rebounding position, but sacrifices face-to-face pressure on perimeter shooters.

Figure 7-2 Illustration of Tall Organization Structure

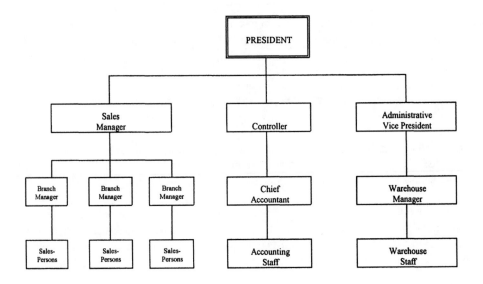

Similarly, a centralized organizational structure has the advantage of a core group of specialists who may have great expertise in their <u>functional</u> area of the business. Yet the disadvantage of this system is that its very advantage may lead to less market-oriented emphasis than under a decentralized system. In addition, it may be difficult to coordinate several functional specialists to perform cooperatively and take a business-wide view.

The decentralized structure has the advantage of a market-oriented, profit-oriented perspective. However, it may suffer from either a lack of functional expertise or require duplication of costs for having the same functional specialists in each division.

Strategic Use of Organizational Structure in Control

In sum, managers wishing to design an appropriate organizational structure must truly make a choice between centralization and decentralization based upon what they wish to accomplish with each control structure. If the principal goal is to motivate people to adopt a profit-orientation, then the decentralized structure is probably appropriate, given that sufficient numbers of strong executives are available to implement it. If the organization consists to a considerable extent of relatively weak players with a few very strong people, then a centralized structure is likely to be superior. This is analogous to the system used to organize a basketball team. The greater the talents of the individual players, the more effective they are likely to be with a man-to-man defense. The less talented teams are more likely to use zone defenses to compensate for a lack of a seven-foot center or relatively large, mobile front-line. A decentralized system tends to be most appropriate when an organization is talent-rich.

It should be noted, of course, that the choice between centralization versus decentralization is not totally an "either-or" decision. These concepts represent two extreme points on a continuum. Some organization structures can be a mixture of centralization and decentralization. For example, a real estate firm can centralize advertising but decentralize sales training; the reverse is also possible.

It is well to recognize that the choice of the degree of centralization or decentralization involves a strategic decision by management about the kind of organization that is desired. This suggests that there are questions concerning the culture of the firm which must be addressed. These issues shall be the focus of the next section.

ROLE OF ORGANIZATIONAL CULTURE IN CONTROL

As used in this context, the term "organizational culture" refers to the system of values, attitudes, and beliefs which prevail within an organization and (explicitly or implicitly) tend to govern the behavior of people.[63] Culture represents written as well as unwritten rules of conduct. It deals with what behavior is expected and what is taboo.

All organizations have a culture, though it may be implicit rather than explicit, and though it may be invisible to non-members. A firm's culture is very real and it must be viewed as a major part of an organization's overall control system.

The Elements of Culture

The three major elements of an organization's culture are values, beliefs and norms. The nature of each variable is described below.

Values. The term "values" refers to the things which the organization's members seek to attain or feel represent the organization. For example, an organization that wants to attain a reputation as the preeminent professional advertising agency, or the "Rolls Royce of consulting firms" is defining itself in a very particular way. Such values govern behavior in a variety of ways. For example, one may hear that the statement in a firm: "We don't do business that way;" or "that wouldn't fit our image;" referring to the firm's self-image as much as its public image.

Most firms have a self-concept which reflects their values. A firm of Certified Public Accountants may see itself as a group of "high quality technically-oriented professionals" or as a group of "good business people." A consumer electronics firm may see itself as a group of hard-driving innovative entrepreneurs, who are willing to assume substantial risks. Another firm in the same industry may view itself as serious, conservative and solid--unwilling to take unnecessary risks.

Beliefs. In brief, a firm's self concept study typically represents its values, or what it is trying to become. Values are accompanied by attitudes and beliefs. One firm may believe in planning as a way of life and develop short term and long term plans. Another firm may believe in continuing management education and development and growing its managers from within. Another may believe that management development is a waste of money, and that if good managers are needed they can be hired. One firm may believe that it must continually innovate new products, while another may believe the pioneers are "people with arrows in their back."

These differences in beliefs are real, if intangible, but they help shape how people in an organization perceive events and design actions. Stated differently, this element of culture influences a manager's set. By simultaneously prescribing "how we do things at IBM Corporation" and influencing how managers perceive things, an organization's belief systems can play a powerful role in controlling behavior. For example, in residential real estate firms, one of the unwritten values is: "Thou shalt always be optimistic." If someone is pessimistic in a meeting, that person is likely to be the object of peer pressure to change his or her view. This may take the form of comments such as: "You're not being very optimistic," or "don't you have faith in your ability to get the job done?"

Norms. The third element of an organization's culture is "norms". This refers to specified modes of prescribed or socially sanctioned behavior. For example, the reputed norm at IBM is for professionals to wear a white shirt, while the reputed norm at certain Silicon Valley electronics firms is <u>not</u> to wear white shirts. At the former, the norm is intended to reinforce the value of professionalism, while at the latter the norm is to reinforce the value of uniqueness and entrepreneurial spirit.

At both companies in the examples above, the norm serves an identical <u>purpose</u>, even though the norms themselves differ. Specifically, each company's norms for dress are intended to buttress the company's values, they way in which people think about themselves.

STRATEGIC USE OF CULTURE IN CONTROL

An organization's culture, <u>per se</u> constitutes a control system. By specifying the kinds of values, beliefs and norms which the organization supports, corporate culture is prescribing and, in turn, controlling behavior.

Although all corporation' have cultures, just as all people have personalities, not all corporations "manage" their culture. By managing its culture, an organization can strategically use it as a component of an overall control system.

The first step in managing corporate culture us to assess what it actually is. Many companies (such as Johnson & Johnson) have "Corporate Credos" which specify their desired culture. However, the actual culture may not coincide with the intended or desired culture. For example, an organization may specify that customer satisfaction is the highest priority while in the actual culture, there may be an indifference or even a subtle contempt for customers. Similarly, the stated culture may emphasize motivation, product quality, and the notion that " people are our most valuable asset," while the actual culture may be quite indifferent to these values.

Management can influence the actual culture by strategically using the organizational reward system, as described in chapter six. The key point is that culture can and does influence the behavior if people in an organization on a daily basis as well as a long term basis.

RELATIONS AMONG CULTURE, STRUCTURE, AND THE
CORE-CONTROL SYSTEM

A firm's culture does not, cannot, and should not exist independently from the other dimensions of its control system. All of the three elements (the core control system, structure, and culture) interact with one another.

To function effectively, all of the firm's three elements of control should operate in concert. This suggests that the three elements <u>ought to be designed as a total system, or a series of interconnected subsystems</u>.

From a normative perspective, the design of the culture variable ought to come first: what the organization values and seeks to become is of paramount importance. The organizational structure ought to be designed in order to help implement the firm's value system, and finally the core-control system ought to be designed to implement the desired culture and structure.

Unfortunately, actual life does not always operate as theory would suggest. More typically, culture is the variable that is recognized last, not first, and any changes required must then be made in previously existing organizational structure and core-control systems.

We shall deal with the design and redesign of actual systems of organizational control and selected examples of the types of problems caused when the three elements of control are not congruent in Chapter 9.

ENDNOTES

59. See Alexander (1991) and Dermer (1987) for other examinations of the role of organizational control systems.
60. For additional information on organizational structure see Bhambri and Sonnenfeld (1988), Capon et al. (1987), Miller et al. (1988), Hoskisson (1987), Shenkar and Ronen (1987), Yasai-Ardekani (1989) and Keats & Hitt (1988).
61. For other discussions on organizational culture see Eisenhardt and Schoonhoven (1990) and Osborn and Baughn (1990).

62. For further discussion organizational structure as a management tool, see Eric G. Flamholtz, Growing Pains: How to Make the Transition from an Entrepreneurship to a Professionally Managed Firm. (Jossey-Bass Publishers, Inc., 1990), pp.184-211.
63. For further discussion of organizational culture, see Ibid, pp.289-318.

REFERENCES

Alexander, J.A., "Adaptive Change in Corporate Control Practices", Academy of Management Journal, 1991, 34:2, 251-280.

Bhambri, A., and H. Sonnenfeld, "Organization Structure and Corporate Social Performance: A Field Study in Two Contrasting Industries", Academy of Management Journal, 1988, 31:3, 642-662.

Capon, A.N., Christodoulou, C., Farley, J.U., and H.M. Hubert, "Comparative Analysis of the Strategy and Structure of U.S. and Australian Corporations, Journal of International Business Studies, 1987, 18:1, 51-74.

Covaleski, M. and M. Aiken, "Accounting and Theories of Organizations: Some Preliminary Considerations", Accounting, Organizations and Society, 1991, 11:4/5, 297-320.

Dent, J.F., "Accounting and Organizational Cultures: A Field Study of the Emergence of a New Organizational Reality, Accounting, Organizations and Society, 1991, 16:8, 705-732.

Dermer, J., "Control and Organizational Order", Accounting, Organizational and Society, 1987, 13:1, 25-36.

Eisenhardt, K.M. and C.B. Schoonhoven, "Organizational Growth: Linking Founding Team, Strategy, Environment and Growth Among U.S. Semiconductor Ventures, 1978-1988", Administrative Sciences Quarterly, 1990, 35, 504-520.

Flamholtz, E. Growing Pains: How to Make the Transition from an Entrepreneurship to an Professionally Managed Firm, Jossey-Bass Publishers, Inc., 1990.

Hoskisson, R.E., "Multidivisional Structure and Performance: The Contingency of Diversification Strategy", Academy of Management Journal, 1987, 30:2, 625-644.

Keats, B.W. and M.A. Hitt, "Causal Model of Linkages Among Environmental Dimensions, Macro Organizational Characteristics", Academy of Management Journal, 1988, 31:3, 570-598.

Miller, D., Droge, C., and J. Toulouse, "Strategic Process and Content as Mediators between Organizational Context and Structure", Academy of Management Journal, 1988, 31:3, 544-569.

Osborn, R.N. and C.C. Baughn, "Forms of Interorganizational Governance for Multinational Alliances", Academy of Management Journal, 1990, 33:2, 503-519.

Shenkar, O. and S. Ronen, "Structure and Importance of Work Goals Among Managers in the People's Republic of China", Academy of Management Journal, 1987, 30:3, 564-576.

Yasai-Ardekani, M., "Effects of Environmental Scarcity and Munificence on the Relationship of Context to Organizational Structure", Academy of Management Journal, 1989, 32:1, 131-156.

8

THE ROLE OF ACCOUNTING SYSTEMS
IN ORGANIZATIONAL CONTROL

Accounting is a system designed to measure, aggregate, and transmit financial data for a variety of managerial purposes. In most organizations, the accounting system is an integral part of the overall core control system because of its measurement capability and the need for measures to facilitate control.

In addition to the role that accounting plays in the overall core control system, certain managerial accounting systems (i.e., budgetary systems) may function as if they were control systems per se. When an accounting system functions as though it were a control system, we may term it as "accounting control system." Accordingly, this section examines the nature of the accounting control system and how it operates as a component of the overall organizational control system. It also examines the principle types of accounting control systems.

DEFINITION OF ACCOUNTING CONTROL SYSTEM

An "accounting control system" may be defined as a set of accounting mechanisms (both techniques and processes) designed to increase the probability that people will behave in says that lead to attainment of organizational objectives. The accounting system has the same ultimate purpose as the overall organizational control system, but it uses different methods.

Traditionally, accounting has been concerned with measuring, processing, and reporting information that can be expressed in monetary terms. More recently, however, the concept of accounting has been evolving to include all quantitative information rather than merely financial data.

Types of Accounting Control Systems

There are three principal types of accounting control systems: 1) budget control systems, 2) responsibility accounting systems, and 3) standard cost-variance control systems. Each of these systems is described below.

BUDGETARY CONTROL SYSTEM

A budgetary control system involves the process of translating overall organizational goals into financial terms (called a "budget"), using the budget derived as a standard or goal of performance, measuring actual performance, and evaluating actual performance vis a vis the budget. The budgetary control system includes goals, standards, and measures, but not rewards. Thus it is technically not a total control system. However, it operates as though it is a control system because budget data ("variances" or deviations from budget) are used as a factor in overall performance-evaluation-reward systems.[64] Stated differently, people tend to pay attention to budget variances even though the budgetary control system does not include extrinsic rewards, because of the use of this information in administering the overall organizational reward system.

The budgetary control system consists of a process and a set of budget reports. The process is the method by which the set of numbers comprising a budget are derived. It may range from a highly participative process of joint decision-making to a relatively autocratic or directive process in which a budget is imposed.

Types of Budgets

Budgets may be developed for several different dimensions of organizational activity, including revenues, expenses, profit, or nonmonetary items such as units of production of time. These dimensions may, in turn, be translated into two types of budgets: 1) fixed budgets or 2) flexible budgets.

A fixed budget is an estimate of some items (sales, costs, etc.) under a single assumption about its level of activity. For example, an automobile manufacturer may assume that it will produce 800,000 passenger cars during a given year, and budget its costs based upon that estimate. Unfortunately, under a fixed budget the attainability of goals becomes meaningless as soon as the actual operating level varies from the level assumed. A flexible budget is a set of budgets, with each prepared under a different assumed level of activity. For example, the automobile manufacturer might prepare production cost budgets under assumptions of minimum, most likely, and maximum units of sales. The flexible budget would then provide a meaningful standard under each possible level of operation, rather than a single hypothetical level.

Behavioral Aspects of Budgetary Control

Once formulated, the budget represents the plans and goals which the organization hopes individuals and groups will achieve. There are three basic budgetary control issues which our knowledge of human behavior can help us resolve:

1. How should the budgetary process be managed in order to motivate people to

internalize the budget as a goal?

2. At what level of difficulty should the budget be set in order to motivate optimal performance?

3. How should organizational rewards be administered in relation to budgetary performance?

Budget as Goals. The organization wants people as individuals or in groups to accept the budgets a goal. According to what we know about human behavior, there is no intrinsic reason for there to be congruence between organizational and individual or group goals.

Individuals pursuing what is best for their own needs may not accept the budget as a goal. They may not perceive that achieving the budget will lead to satisfaction of their goals. For an individual to be motivated to achieve the budget, he of she must, first, perceive that the achievement of the budget is instrumental for the attainment of some desired outcome or set of outcomes, and, second, place a positive value on those outcomes. Thus the acceptance of the budget as an individual's goal is a question of personal rationality.

Similarly, groups may or may not accept a budget as a goal. Subgroup loyalty may lead to conflict between the goal of a group and the organization as a whole. Such conflict may be manifest not in the rejection of the budget as a goal per se, but in intergroup conflict and competition for budget resources. For example, Division A may compete with Division B to maximize its share of the budget pie, rather than to obtain a budget that would merely be sufficient to satisfy its needs. This may be quite rational from the vantage point of Division A's personnel, because their performance will depend upon the resources available to them including "slack." A great deal of political behavior may result from this motivation, causing intergroup competition.

The budgeting process can serve as a mechanism to facilitate the integration of individual, group, and organizational goals. Budgeting is an iterative process through which conflicts between subgroups can be resolved by negotiation and compromise. Indeed, it is likely that bargaining and compromise take precedence over analytical efforts in deriving a budget. Thus the budgeting process may result in subjective rationality (rationality according to the needs of organizational participants) rather than economic rationality according to organizational criteria.

Budgets as Standards. In thinking about budgeting as a control system, we should distinguish between the budget as a goal and the standard of performance that underlies a particular budget. An individual may accept achievement of a budget as a general goal, but the degree of difficulty of a specific standard implied by a budget may or may not be accepted as a person's level of aspiration. For example, a manager may accept the notion that one of his goals is to achieve budgeted profit, while he or she may feel that a budgeted profit of 25% of sales before taxes is too difficult to achieve.

The organization wants people to accept budgets as their levels of aspiration. The degree to which this will occur depends upon the perceived degree of difficulty of the budget, whether it is perceived as realistic and attainable, and the perceived relation of performance to organizational rewards.

If an individual perceives that a budget is too difficult to attain of totally unrealistic, the person will not internalize the budget as a level of aspiration. In terms of expectancy theory, the perceived difficulty of the budget affects the expectancy of the person that effort will lead to budget achievement. In addition, past experience of performance in relation to budgets also serves as an input to a person to formulate expectancies.

Another factor affecting the acceptance of a budget as a performance standard or level of aspiration is group norms. If a person's peer group accepts of rejects the budget as a standard, this is likely to impact the person. The greater the degree of group cohesiveness, the more likely group norms are to influence an individual's acceptance of the budget.

One organizational method of inducing individuals and groups to accept budgeted levels as their aspirations is through the rewards offered. Rewards such as pay, promotions, etc. are intended to affect the valences of people. This will be examined in the section on the budgetary evaluation-reward system.

Another method for attempting to induce internalization is the style of management or leadership used in the budgetary process. It should be noted at the outset that there is no one style of management of leadership that is likely to be most effective in managing the budgetary process; rather, the choice of a style is contingent (depends) upon several factors, including the nature of the budgetary task, the personalities of people involved, the organizational climate, etc.

The primary issue of leadership or management style involved here concerns the degree of participation of people responsible for achieving the budget in the establishment of budgeted standards. There is a great deal of research which suggests that participation leads to greater commitment to organizational goals.

Although it is clear that the desire for participation in decisions depends upon personality and not all individuals desire to participate, it is possible hat participation in the budgetary process can serve as a method of helping to induce internalization of a budget. However, it should also be noted that if the process is more than a pseudo or spurious process, then standards ultimately set may not necessarily be identical to what the organization might set in the absence of participation. For example, some organizations budget costs by merely issuing notices that budgets will be X per cent more or less than the prior year. The percentage change does not necessarily come from a participative budgeting process.

Budget Performance Measurement. The measurement dimension of budgetary control is provided by budget reports. There are two principal purposes of budget reports: 1) to provide feedback on actual versus planned performance, and 2) to provide a basis for evaluating performance.

The basic measure of budgetary performance is the variance. Budget variances represent deviations from plans. Algebraically, Variance = Budget - Actual. Variances may be "favorable" or "unfavorable." For example, favorable variance can occur in a sales budget when actual sales are greater than budgeted sales, or in an expense budget when actual costs are less than budgeted costs.

An important managerial problem in budgetary control is the interpretation of budget variances. Although variances are intended to measure performance, they cannot be accepted as valid without further analysis. In interpreting variances, it is important to determine whether: 1) they are controllable or uncontrollable, or 2) material or insignificant.

Some activities may be included in a budget which are not truly subject to the control of the person responsible for the budget. One accounting practice is to "allocate" (distribute by means of cost accounting methods) the costs of common of joint activities to individual units which are thought to benefit indirectly. For example, costs of corporate headquarters may be allocated to divisions, or costs of the personnel functions may be allocated to other departments. From the perspective of management control, this practice is not beneficial. Such costs are not subject to control of the organizational unit to which they are allocated, and if this is not recognized it can have dysfunctional (adverse) results. Managers may begin to question the validity of the budgetary control system, or may be misled by the numbers in the budget reports.

Another reason why not all variances ought to be investigated involves materiality. It is not possible to a general criterion or cutoff for insignificant versus significant variances. This depends upon the nature of the industry and the item. For example, a 1% (or possibly less) variance in materials cost in the tobacco industry may be very significant, while a 5% of even 10% variance in labor colt in the petro-chemical industry may be insignificant. Nevertheless, some criterion must be developed that is valid for the particular situation.

Budget Evaluation and Rewards. The primary function of the evaluation-reward aspect of budgetary control is to provide the Ex Ante motivation to achieve the budget and the Ex Post reinforcement necessary to ensure future motivation. The budget evaluation is typically based upon the analysis of variances. Thus it is extremely important that the variances be valid or perceived as valid measures of performance.

In general, only controllable activities in the budget ought you be used as the bases for evaluation and reinforcement of budget performance. If an individual does not perceive that performance is controllable, then, in terms of expectancy theory, the person's perception that effort will lead to performance will be decreased.

RESPONSIBILITY ACCOUNTING

Responsibility accounting is a philosophy of attempting to control organizational behavior by: 1) assigning responsibility (or accountability) for financial activities to specified organizational subunits, 2) measuring the performance of those units, and 3) reporting the performance to these persons assigned responsibility as well as to those who supervise them. The generic idea of responsibility accounting pervades other types of accounting control systems (i.e., budgeting and standard costing), rather that existing as a system per se. In brief, any accounting system that is used to assign responsibility, measure and report on performance may be referred to as a responsibility accounting system. There are, however, some concepts and ideas that comprise a theory of responsibility accounting that ought to be viewed independently of the techniques used.

Motivational Basis of Responsibility Accounting

The fundamental idea underlying responsibility accounting is that tasks con be subdivided into units for which people may be held responsible, and, in turn, the individuals responsible for the task will be motivated to perform the required responsibilities. An implicit premise is that the motivation to perform such responsibilities is extrinsic, and is aroused by holding individuals accountable, measuring their performance, and providing evaluative feedback. At present, a well developed theory of responsibility accounting and its behavioral effects does not exist. This is a fruitful area for future research.

The traditional responsibility accounting approach is based upon the motivation of individuals rather than groups. Individuals are treated as the basic unit of responsibility.

Responsibility Centers. The basic unit of control under responsibility accounting is a "responsibility center" headed by an individual. A "responsibility center" is an organizational unit to which a specified set of tasks (responsibilities) have been assigned.

There are several types of responsibility centers, including 1) investment centers, 2) profit centers, and 3) cost centers. An "investment center" is a responsibility center in which the person(s) responsible have control over (the authority to make decisions involving) revenues, costs, and capital investment. For example, the General Electric

Corporation as a whole may be viewed as an investment center, but some of its divisions may not, where they fail to have the authority for capital expenditures (investment). A "profit center" is an organizational unit which has control over both revenues and expenses, but <u>not</u> investment. For example, The Chevrolet Unit of General Motors might be a profit center (not an investment center) if it controls revenues and expenses but not capital investment. A "cost center" is an organizational unit which has control over costs but not revenues or expenses. For example, a manufacturing plant that produces a product based on orders from an independent sales unit is a cost center; it controls its manufacturing costs but not revenues. Similarly, the accounting department of a corporation is a cost center.

There are two major types of cost centers: 1) Engineered Cost Centers and 2) Discretionary Cost Centers. The former is a cost center in which it is possible to utilize industrial engineering to determine what costs ought to be ("standard costs") under specified operating conditions. In such centers, such as certain manufacturing organizations, these standard costs can be used for control, as examined below In the latter, it is not possible to determine what costs should be and there is no obvious relationship between inputs and outputs. Costs are thus subject to management's judgement or discretion. Hence the name "discretionary costs centers."

STANDARD COST-VARIANCE CONTROL SYSTEMS

A standard cost-variance control system involves the process of determining what costs ought to be under specified operating conditions, using the cost derived as a standard and goal of performance, measuring actual performance, and evaluating actual performance vis a vis the standard cost. A standard cost-variance control system is closely related to a budgetary control system. Both include goals, standards, and measures, but not rewards. Similarly, while both are not technically total control systems, they operate with the effect of control systems because variances are used in performance evaluation.

Definition of Standard Costs

A standard cost is a calculation of what costs for an activity or item <u>ought to be</u> under predetermined operating conditions. It is then a normative or hypothetical cost. As the title implies, it is intended as a standard for evaluating the efficiency of operations.

Standard costing developed initially as a technique for control over manufacturing operations. More recently, however, it has been applied in service organizations to many aspects of operations. For example, it can be applied in the operations of banks of insurance companies, which provide services rather than manufacturing goods.

Standard costs may be established through engineering and/or accounting studies. If engineering methods are used, detailed analyses are made of the tasks which must be performed to provide a service of produce a good, their optimal or "standard" sequence and duration id specified as will as materials required (if any), and the cost of the direct labor and materials as will as overhead (indirect materials, labor, and services) is calculated. Alternately, accounting records may be used to determine what an activity or product has cost historically and this historical cost may be employed as a standard.

Types of Variances

Several different types of variances may be calculated under a standard costing system. The basic variances are shown in summary in Figure 8-1.

There are two basic classes of variances: 1) acquisition cost variances refer to the variances between the standard cost of acquiring cost variances refer to the variances between the standard cost of acquiring an input for operations (labor, material for overhead) and the actual cost incurred. As seen in Figure 8-1, the acquisition cost variance for materials is called a "price variance." For example, if the standard price of a raw material used in manufacturing chemicals is .20 pound, and the actual cost is .22 per pound, a price variance will be incurred that is measured by multiplying the differential cost (.22 - .20 =.02) by the number of pounds of the material that are purchased. If 100,000 pounds ore purchased, the materials price variance is $2,000. Similarly, acquisition cost variances may be calculated for labor and overhead, though different labels are used to denote them. Utilization colt variances refer to the variances between the standard cost of using an input in an operation to produce a good or service and the actual cost incurred.[65]

	MATERIALS	**LABOR**	**OVERHEAD**
Acquisition Cost Variances	Price Variance	Rate Variance	Spending Variance
Utilization Variances	Quantity Variance	Efficiency Variance	Efficiency Variance Volume Variance

Figure 8-1
Summary of Basic Variances

Behavioral Aspects of Standard Cost Control

In general, the basic issue involving the control of human behavior with standard costs are quite similar to those concerning budgetary control. The four primary issues are:

1. How should standard costs be set in order to motivate their acceptance or internalization as a performance goal?
2. At what level of difficulty should a standard be set in order to motivate optimal performance?
3. How should variances be interpreted in evaluating performance?
   and
4. How should organizational rewards be administered in relation to performance against standard costs?

In many respects standard costs variance controls operate in the same ways as budgetary controls. Accordingly, to avoid repetition, this section will emphasize those aspects which are relatively unique to standard costing.

Standard Costs as Goals and Standards. The idea underlying standard costing as a control tool is very consistent with the overall notion of organizational control. By definition, the purpose of standard costs is to serve as a goal to motivate cost control as well as a specific standard of performance against that goal.

Just as in the case of budgets, neither individuals nor groups will necessarily accept cost control as their goals. There are four basic prerequisites for a "behaviorally sound" control system: 1) standards must be established in a way that people accept them as realistic rather than arbitrary; 2) people must feel that they have some influence in establishing their own goals; 3) people must feel that they will not be unfairly censured for "normal" of chance variation in performance; and 4) feedback on performance must be for both correction as well as evaluation.

Standards must be perceived as realistic in order to be accepted as a person's level of aspiration and to motivate optimal performance. Drawing upon what we know about the effects of perceived task difficulty on performance, to experience success or failure a person must perceive that a task is difficult but attainable. If a task is perceived as extremely difficult or impossible, a person may not internalize it as a level of aspiration and, in turn, may not strive to attain it. The result is that an extremely difficult task may actually elicit less motivation and lower performance than a somewhat easier, more attainable task. For these reasons, it is generally believed that a realistic, somewhat difficult, but attainable standard should be used in order to motivate optimal performance.

The process of establishing standards can play a crucial role in the degree to which they are accepted as realistic and attainable. The traditional methods of establishing standard costs (engineering and accounting estimates), described above, do not typically provide an opportunity for individuals to participate in their development. Yet participation is a major managerial strategy designed to lead to commitment to organizational goals and standards. Thus we must recognize the built in conflict between what is psychologically necessary in order to have people internalize goals and the way in which standard costs are established in most organizations. This suggests the need for some mechanism to permit people to participate in setting standards. In many industries, unions negotiate work standards with management and indirectly serve the function of legitimizing standards.

Standard Cost Performance Measurement. The measurement dimension of standard cost control is provided by reports comparing actual costs with standard costs and calculating the variances. The same concepts and ideas are relevant for standard cost variances as for budget variances, and will not be repeated here.

Standard Cost Evaluation. Just as for performance measurement, the analysis of standard cost variances is quite similar to the process for budgeting, and will not be repeated. Both budgetary and standard cost control systems utilize variances as their criterion for performance evaluation.

CONCLUSION

This chapter has examined the nature of accounting control techniques and their role as part of the overall organizational control systems. Budgetary systems, responsibility accounting systems, and standard cost systems all function, to some extent, as accounting control systems. However, from a technical standpoint, they are not fully control systems. Nevertheless, accounting systems can serve a significant role as part of an overall control system.

ENDNOTES

64. A "variance" is operationally defined as: Variance = Budget - Actual
65. For further discussion of standard costing and variance analysis see Buckley and Lightner (1975) Chapter 16.

REFERENCES

Birnberg, J.G. and C. Snodgrass, "Culture and Control: A Field Study", <u>Accounting, Organizations and Society</u>, 1988, 13:5, 447-464.

Buckley, J.W. and K. Lightner, <u>Essentials of Accounting</u>, (Encino, CA: Dickenson Publishing Co., 1975).

Daley, L., Jiambalvo, J., Sundem, G., and Y. Kondo, "Attitudes Toward Financial Control Systems in the U.S. and Japan", <u>Journal of International Business Studies</u>, 1985, 16:3, 91-110.

Dent, J.F., "Accounting and Organizational Cultures: A Field Study of the Emergence of a New Organizational Reality", <u>Accounting, Organizations and Society</u>, 1991, 16:82, 705-732.

Flamholtz, E., <u>Human Resource Accounting</u>, (San Francisco, CA: Jossey-Bass Publishers, Inc., 1985).

Jones, C.S., "The Attitudes of Owner-Managers Towards Accounting Control Systems Following Management Buyout", <u>Accounting, Organizations and Society</u>, 1992, 17:2, 151-168.

Kerr, S., "On the Folly of Rewarding A, While Hoping for B," <u>Academy of Management Journal</u>, (December, 1975), pp. 769-783.

Lawler, E.E. and J.G. Rhode, <u>Information and Control in Organizations</u>, (Pacific Palisades, CA: Goodyear Publishing Co., 1976).

Merchant, K.A., "The Effects of Financial Controls on Data Manipulation and Management Myopia", <u>Accounting, Organizations and Society</u>, 1990, 15:4, 297-314.

9

THE DESIGN AND EVALUATION OF EFFECTIVE CONTROL SYSTEMS

Previous chapters have been concerned with the nature and role of organizational control, the effects of control on behavior, the elements of an overall control system, and the accounting-control system as a component of the overall organizational control system. This final chapter deals with some aspects of the design and evaluation of control systems in organizations. Specifically, it focuses upon the criteria which can be used to guide the development on evaluation of an existing control system. It also examines the adverse or dysfunctional effects of control systems that have not been effectively designed. Finally, we shall examine selected examples of control systems in order to illustrate their strengths and weaknesses. In brief, the overall objective of the chapter is to provide a framework that can be useful in the design and evaluation of control systems in order to enhance their effectiveness.

CRITERIA OF EFFECTIVE CONTROL SYSTEMS

By definition, the ultimate criterion of an effective control system is the extent to which it increases the probability that people will behave in ways that lead to the attainment of organizational objectives. Thus, since the objective of a control system is to promote goal congruence, an identity between the goals of organizational members (individuals as well as groups) and the organization as a whole, the criterion of an effective control system is the extent to which it creates goals congruence. If a control system does not lead to goal congruence, it is not effective. Alternatively, if a control system sometimes leads to goal congruence but sometimes leads to goal conflict, it is also ineffective, or at least less effective than might be desired.

To achieve overall goal congruence, a control system must also satisfy certain penultimate and instrumental criteria:

1. To what extent does the system seek to control all relevant goals or aspects of performance?
2. To what extent does the system lead to behaviors to which it is intended to (or purports to) lead? and
3. To what extent does the system consistently lead to the same behaviors?

The first of these criteria may be viewed as a penultimate goal or criterion of control systems, while the second and third are instrumental criteria. This is shown schematically in Figure 9-1.

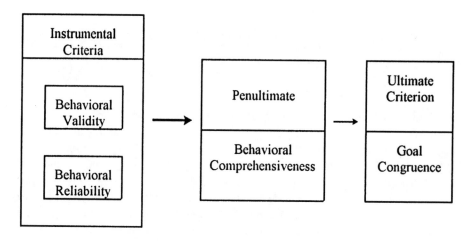

Figure 9-1
Criteria of Effective Control Systems

Behavioral Comprehensiveness

To be effective, a control system must identify all relevant behaviors or goals which are required by the organization. This is termed "behavioral comprehensiveness." If the system does not identify all relevant goals and seek to control them, then people may simply channel their efforts toward some other direction. For example, a university may desire to achieve both the goals of research and education, but may only have a control system that deals with the goal of research. Thus the system monitors and rewards research while hoping for attention to education as well.

A lack of behavioral comprehensiveness is probably the most common weakness found in actual organizational control systems. Typically we find organizations while purport to seek several goals simultaneously, but which have designed core control systems that focus on only some areas while ignoring others. The results are predictable: people pay attention to those areas in which there are goals, standards, measures, evaluations and rewards and tend to ignore or, at least, minimize the rest. We shall examine this problem more fully in this section, including an illustration of an actual control system, presented subsequently.

Behavioral Validity

This construct refers to the extent to which an organizational control system leads to behaviors to which it purports to lead (intended behavior). For example, a control system may be desired to motivate attention to achieving a budgeted profit <u>and</u> personnel development. If the system leads to these behaviors that are in conflict with these goals (unintended behaviors), it is behaviorally invalid. In general, a control system cannot be expected to lead to behaviors that are totally consistent with what is desired, and we must therefore, strive for a satisfactory degree of behavioral validity.

The concept of "behavioral validity" is based upon the recognition that the purpose of a control system is to influence human behavior. This notion has important and somewhat subtle implications for the design of control systems. For example, assume that a CEO (chief executive officer) wants to motivate his or her line management to devote efforts toward the development of personnel and especially to develop their own successors. The CEO might state at an annual management meeting: "One of our goals is developing people and because it is one of our goals we will measure the change in value of people by using Human Resource Accounting.[66] We will also take this factor into account in our appraisal of managerial performance."

In effect, the CEO of this company has described a key result area (Human Resource Development) and an implicit core control system, with the components of planning (goals), measurement, and evaluation-reward. If this "system" is successful in leading to increased personnel development, then we say it has "behavioral validity," even if the "system" per se is vague, ambiguous, and not well defined.

In practice, however, this type of informal or implicit core control system may lead some managers to develop people while not motivating others to do so. This refers to the control system's consistency or reliability, as defined below.

Behavioral Reliability

This is the extent to which a control system repeatedly produces the same behaviors regardless of whether these behaviors are intended or unintended. A control system which produces the same behavior in all managers or the same behavior in the same manager over different times is termed behaviorally reliable or consistent.

Behavioral reliability is more likely to occur when the control system has been specified to a greater extent than in the example of the CEO's comments at an annual management meeting.

Behavioral reliability is different from and is not sufficient without behavioral validity. A control system may have a high degree of behavioral reliability, but it may lead consistently to unintended, dysfunctional behaviors.

Goal Displacement

This involves a lack of goal congruence created by motivation to achieve some goals sought by the organization at the expense of other intended goals. Goal displacement may be caused by several things, including 1) suboptimization, 2) selective attention to goals, and 3) inversion of means and ends.

Suboptimization. Suboptimization occurs when the performance of an organizational subunit is optimized at the expense of the organization as a whole. For example, a control system may be intended to contribute to profit, and may seek to control manufacturing efficiency by means of standard costing. Management may reward performance based upon variance measurement. However, unintended consequences of this control system may occur. It may lead persons responsible for standard costs to concentrate upon their measured performance, at the expense of other organizational goals such as sales revenues for which they are not responsible. Persons responsible for manufacturing cost centers may be reluctant or unwilling to modify production schedules to accommodate special customer requests, because of the effects of such changes upon manufacturing costs. From the perspective of the manufacturing subunit, this is rational behavior because their goal is manufacturing efficiency, rather than profit per se. The suboptimization is caused by factoring overall organizational goals into subgoals and holding individuals and units responsible for those subgoals. It is a common problem and difficult to avoid in large complex organizations. Stated differently, it is caused because the control system for the subunit lacks total behavioral relevance; that is, not all required behaviors are controlled.

Selective Attention. Another type of goal displacement is caused by selective attention to organizational goals. This is closely related to suboptimization, and occurs when certain goals of the organization are pursued selectively while other goals receive less attention or are ignored. For example, a Certified Public Accounting (CPA) firm may wish to achieve both current profitability and employee development. Yet the control system may monitor the former but not the latter. Thus managers may be motivated to maximize contribution to profit even at the expense of not developing personnel. The control system contributes to this problem by measuring contribution to profit but not employee development. One possible solution is to measure both of these dimensions and include them in performance evaluation. Recognition of this problem has, in part, led to the development of "Human Resource Accounting."[67] Measures of changes in human resource value might be used in assessing management's attention to this aspect of performance.

Similarly, the sales manager of an automobile dealership, who was rewarded based upon sales but was not responsible for costs, unreasonably increased expenditures for advertising even though it was unprofitable for the dealership to do so.

Means-Ends Inversion. A third type of goal displacement is caused by the inversion of means and ends. This occurs when a control system tries to motivate attention to certain instrumental goals, which become ends in themselves for people because they are rewarded. This illustrated, for example, in the case of a public agency whose major goal was to serve workers seeking employment and employers seeking workers. The tasks to be performed included interviewing applicants, helping them to complete application forms, counseling them, and referring them to jobs. To control the interviewers, the agency monitored the number of interviews conducted. The effect of this control system was to motivate the interviewers to pay attention to the instrumental goals (i.e., numbers of interviews), while neglecting the overall (but unmeasured) goal of placing people in jobs.

Measurement

This involves a lack of goal congruence created by motivation to "look good" in terms of the measures used in control systems, even though no real benefit has derived to the organization. It involves playing "the numbers game" and manipulating the measures used by a control system. There are two primary types of measurementship: 1) smoothing and 2) falsification.

"Smoothing" refers to an attempt to time activities in such a way as to offer the appearance of measures in different time periods. All measures used in control systems relate to specified time periods. We may wish to control units of production or net income for a month or year. A manager may wish to smooth the calculated net income number in two adjacent periods (i.e., 19x8 and 19x9). This can be accomplished, for example, if profit is expected to be unusually high during 19x8 by incurring expenditures that would have been made in 19x9 in the prior year.

Falsification refers to reporting invalid data about what is occurring in an organization. The invalid data is designed to make a person or an activity "look good" in terms of the measurement system.

ILLUSTRATIONS OF CONTROL SYSTEMS

The preceding section has presented a set of criteria for designing and evaluating effective control systems and discussed the problems caused by ineffective control systems. In this next section, we shall examine selected examples of control systems in order to illustrate some of their strengths and weaknesses as well as some of the problems typically observed in actual systems of organizational control.

Specifically, we shall examine three different types of common situations:

1. Organizations in which there is no formal system of organizational control;
2. Organizations with a formal system of control dealing with only some of the key result areas; and
3. Organizations in which the firm's culture and the core control system are not synchronized.

Each of these types of situations shall be described in order to examine their effects on organizational control.

Control in Absence of Formal Control Systems

There are many firms which operate without a formal control system as it has been described in this book. Typically such firms are relatively small (sales less than $10 million). However, occasionally even large firms have not developed formal control systems. Such firms will have elements of a control system but <u>not</u> a complete system.

In this section, we shall examine one relatively small firm that operates without a formal control system and explain why this was so and describe the regretting difficulties.

Nature of the Firm. The firm in question was an industrial abrasives distributor. The firm distributed a full set of industrial abrasive products to industrial firms which use the products in their own manufacturing process. We shall term this firm "Industrial Abrasives, Inc."

Industrial Abrasives, Inc. had its major facility located in a large metropolitan city in the U.S. The firm also had one satellite branch office in another major city. The firm's sales volume exceeded $12 million annually, and the firm employed approximately 75 persons.

Firm's Culture, Structure, and Accounting System. Although the firm had been founded more than twenty years prior to this study, for most of its history it had remained relatively small in terms of sales volume and personnel. During the past few years, the firm had experienced rapid growth in sales volume attributable to favorable economic conditions, its full range of products, sales force, and ability to meet customer service requirements. During a three year period the firm increased in size from $3 ½ million to more than $12 million.

The firm was owned by a single family, and three family members (a father and two sons) ran the firm along with other family members. As typical in firms of this size, responsibilities were not formally defined and tended to be overlapping.

The firm had been successful, at least in part, because of competitively priced products and skill at selling by family members and the sales staff. None of the members of the family as well as virtually all other "managers" had been formally trained in management. The firm did have a "Controller," who was a CPA.

The Accounting System and Organization Control. The firm did not have any formal system of management control as it has been defined in this monograph. As an organizational function, "control" was exercised by the personal involvement of family members in the day-to-day activities of the firm, rather than through formal planning, measurement, performance appraisal and reward systems. In this respect, the firm was probably quite typical of most organizations with its type of history: rapid growth as an entrepreneurship.

The firm's accounting system produced an annual income statement and balance sheet. An illustrative income statement is shown in Exhibit 9-1 to indicate the format used; the numbers have been eliminated. These financial statements were prepared at the end of each year to determine the firm's yearly income and financial position both for ownership and tax purposes; but they were not used otherwise in day-to-day management of the business.

As seen in Exhibit 9-1, the income statement format is very simple. Expenses are listed alphabetically rather than by functional categories (selling, administrative, warehouse, etc.). Although the firm has four different product lines, there is no attempt at product line profitability analysis, and this did not occur in any other way in the firm. Indeed, management did not know what the relative product line profitability was except in terms of "gross margin": selling price less direct materials costs. In neither this income statement nor any supplementary analysis was there any attempt to classify costs as "fixed or variable, controllable or uncontrollable." As noted above, the income statement was prepared annually and, therefore was not available for periodic monitoring during the year. In addition there was no budget or profit plan. Thus, there was neither an attempt to set profit goals nor to assess the variance of actual profit in relation to goals.

In brief, there was not a formal system or control in this firm, an the accounting system did not perform any of the control functions ordinarily associated with it. Indeed, the firm's financial statements were virtually ignored except to determine whether or not a profit had been made.

If this organization's firm were merely an illustration of an isolated firm that lacked sophisticated management, it would be of little significance. However, this firm is a classic illustration of an entrepreneurship that has experienced rapid growth and has not yet responded to its changed circumstances. Rather than being a-typical, it is the prototype of a great many successful firms of its size in a variety of industries. As such, it suggests significant insights for our understanding of the actual role (or more properly, lack of a role) that accounting plays in its organizational context in a great many firms.

Impact of Culture Upon Utilization of Accounting and Control. What explains the firm's lack of formal organizational control system as well as its failure to use accounting information to facilitate organizational control? The key is in the organization's culture.

The firm is an entrepreneurship. It was successful because it could do certain

Exhibit 9-1   Industrial Abrasives, Inc.:   Income Statement Before Income Taxes

Year Ending September 30,

Sales
Cost of Goods Sold

    GROSS PROFIT ON SALES

OPERATING EXPENSES:

Advertising
Bad Debt Provision
Car Expense
Commissions
Contributions
Data Processing Service
Depreciation
Entertainment
Freight Out
Insurance - Officer's Life
Insurance - General
Insurance - Group
Interest
Medical and Dental
Office Expense
Postage
Professional Fees
Profit Sharing
Rent
Repairs and Maintenance
Salaries - Officers, Manager
Salaries - Office
Salaries - Sales
Salaries - Warehouse
Shipping Supplies
Taxes - Payroll
Taxes and Licenses
Telephone
Travel
Utilities

    TOTAL OPERATING EXPENSES
    INCOME FROM OPERATIONS
    OTHER INCOME   (EXPENSE)
    INCOME BEFORE INCOME TAXES

operational things very well: buy product, sell it, deliver it, and service customers. Personal attention to the business and an open-ended commitment by family members and many employees made the firm prosper and grow. However, the firm lacked a professional management orientation. It did no formal planning, and there was not even informal long range planning; rather, the firm reacted to changing events and circumstances. Organizational roles were not defined explicitly. People did what work had to be done. There was no budget, but the controller paid attention to cash flow. Because the firm was growing, sales revenues were sufficient to cover expenses, and the firm had a line of credit sufficient to cover short-term cash requirements.

The firm was sales and product-oriented. Its owners were skilled in personal selling and because of good interpersonal skills they were also able to maintain relations with suppliers. If expenses had to be increased, the culture responded, explicitly and implicitly, by saying "So we'll have to go out and get some more business." Indeed, when a profit budget had been prepared for the first time, and the president was advised of a projected loss the possibility of personnel layoffs was proposed. The president responded: "Why don't we just go out and get some more business." Although this response was quite typical, it was not appropriate to the current economic environment.

Consequences of Lack of Control System. What were the consequences of the lack of a formal control system for this firm? For most of its history, the firm was able to operate profitably without a formal control system, but there was an opportunity cost. As the firm began to increase its sales revenues rapidly, profits remained surprisingly level. In effect, the firm had increased its volume but had not increased profitability correspondingly. The cost of a lack of a formal control system was less profit than the firm ought to have earned.

As long as market conditions were good, the problem of lack of control remained an opportunity cost and hence was intangible. However, the firm began to feel the effects of a wide-spread economic decline in the U.S. and, for the first time, as stated above, faced a projected loss. At this point, the firm had already begun to try and develop a formal control system but it was too late, and the cost of not having moved quickly enough to accommodate changed needs was now more severe.

Conclusions. As illustrated by this firm's history, formal control systems are not always essential to a firm's profitability and survival. However, after a certain size is reached ($10 million or more in sales), the lack of a formal control system can become an acute problem.

Control in the Absence of Behavioral Comprehensiveness

There are many firms which do have formal control systems but which have systems dealing with only some of the organization's key result areas. The problems encountered by such firms are different from those experienced by firms with no formal control system. This section describes an example of a firm that has a formal control system which leads to selective attention to organizational goals because of the failure to include all relevant key result areas. This type of problem is especially important today in U.S. organizations.

Nature of the Organization. The organization is a manufacturing plant which produces glass containers and jars. It is a division of a large multi-national firm.

The plant is treated as a cost center and has a standard cost system used in connection with cost control. Top management states that the key areas of concern for plant management are: cost control, product quality, timeliness of product delivery, and safety.

The firm has a formal system of planning and control, and year-end bonuses are paid for achieving manufacturing efficiency ratings.

Problems with Control System. There has been increasing evidence of customer dissatisfaction during the past few years. The firm's sales force reports customer complaints about product quality and missed delivery dates. Sales personnel also complain that plant personnel are no sufficiently sensitive to customer needs, and that there is an unwillingness to modify production schedules to accommodate large rush orders. Plant personnel encounter that they are evaluated upon plan efficiency measures derived from the standard costing system and they are just doing what the firm wants them to do -- be as efficient as possible.

Analysis of Control Problems. The key problems facing this firm are suboptimization and goal displacement. The plant is optimizing its manufacturing efficiency measurements because the control system is effective in motivating the behavior it is designed to produce. However, other important but uncontrolled variables are not receiving sufficient attention including product quality and timeliness of delivery. This occurs because the formal control system is limited to financial variables and does not include these other factors.

This plant is a classic illustration of the problems facing a great many U.S. manufacturing firms, caused by ineffectively designed core control systems. The solution is to correct the system to increase the degree of behavioral comprehensiveness so that all key result variables are under control.

Problems When Culture and Core Control Systems Are Not Synchronized

Our final example concerns the problems caused when an organization's culture and its core control system are not sufficiently synchronized. Stated differently, what happens when there is an inconsistency between what the organization's culture says it wants and what is motivated and rewarded by the core control system?

This type of problem is common even in relatively large, well-managed firms. Our example is drawn from a professional service firm.

Problems of Partial Control in a CPA Firm. This firm is a major international firm of Certified Public Accountants (CPAs). It provides a wide variety of audit, tax, and consulting services for clients. The firm is professionally managed and profitable. It has a strategic plan, and a formal control system.

The basic control problem experienced by the firm is in the "Human Resources" key result area. The Human Resources area is an explicit part of the firm's strategic plan and there are specific goals in the firm's strategic plan dealing with the recruitment, development, and retention of people.

The control problem facing the firm is that its human resource goals are not being fulfilled. The major explanation for this problem is that the firm's formal control system is not sufficiently synchronized with its culture.

Analysis of Control Problem. This firm has a formal organizational control system. The firm has an annual planning process and sets goals for all relevant key result areas. The firm also has an evaluation process which purports to assess partner performance in all key areas, including the human resources area.

The six key result areas in which partners are evaluated are: 1) Client relations, 2) Development and motivation of others, 3) Practice development, 4) Practice management, 5) Self-development, and 6) Technical effectiveness. These areas purport to represent the firm's value system, its culture.

On paper, all of these key result areas are equally important. However, the real value system of the firm is reflected in the administration of the partner evaluation process. In this process, what gets measured and rewarded gets attention paid by partners. In terms of the firm's culture, if no one gets "gigged" (penalized) for <u>not</u> developing people or <u>not</u> developing practice, then sufficient motivation will not be focused upon these variables.

In brief, the firm <u>says</u> it wants personnel development, but it does not reward people for personnel development and it does not punish (gig) people for failing to develop people. The firm <u>says</u> it wants technical effectiveness and it rewards partners (through compensation and promotion) for technical effectiveness, while punishing people for inadequate technical effectiveness. Thus it is not surprising that the firm is perceived as technically effective but inadequate in its development and retention of people.

This is another example that the process of organizational control is not magical or mysterious. The control system does what it is "told" to do. It produces the behavior it is <u>designed</u> to produce even if this differs from what top management <u>says</u> it wants.

THE OVERALL CONTROL SYSTEM

The previous section of this chapter has examined selected problems of control systems which are commonly observed in actual organizations.   In this final section, we shall examine an example of the overall core control system. Our purpose is to present a "mini" case study of the issue, involving the effective functioning of a core control system.

Superior Alarm Systems

Superior Alarm Systems is a rapidly growing distributor and installer of electronic alarm systems for automobiles. The firm was originally founded in the early 1980s as "an electronics boutique," where individuals could purchase stereo systems, alarm systems, and other electronic devices for installation in automobiles.   With demographic changes, the firm noted a rapid growth in market for original equipment or replacement alarm systems, and by 1985 had totally redirected their focus to just the installation of these electronic systems.

The original location of the firm was a single store in a major metropolitan area in a large western state. The firm emphasized a variety of competitive aspects, including the use of original equipment, materials, competitive prices, rapid service, quality of installation, and field service by means of radio dispatched trucks. As the firm began to grow, it targeted new geographical markets. By 1986 the firm had organized a franchise operation, and had established ten locations throughout the state. Each of the franchises is organized with a branch manager, a number of installation technicians, and an administrative assistant. The administrative assistant's function is critical to the effectiveness of the operation of the branch since they had the primary contact with the customer, and are required to relay most of the critical information concerning sales and or repairs. The installation and repair technicians are also critical to the effective operation of the firm. Incorrect installation or faulty repair creates significant customer ill will and substantial cost to the company. The "branch manager" is actually an owner/operator, who has an investment in the franchise. Depending upon the size of the branch the branch manager may also function simultaneously as an installer/technician or even as a sales person. Some of the larger branches, there may be one or more full time sales personnel.

By 1989, the firm had grown to approximately $25 million in annual revenue. The firm was growing at an average rate of 22 percent a year, and because of rapid growth both in terms of the number of branch operations, as well as in the total volume of sales there had been relatively little time to develop the infrastructure of the organization.

Development of Control Systems

Certain aspects of the Superior Alarm control systems were more developed than others. The company had developed a relatively sophisticated strategic planning process. The firm had been involved in numerous formal planning exercises over several years since its inception. The planning meetings involved a considerable amount of discussion generating ideas concerning problems facing the company, identifying alternatives, assessing the strengths and limitations, searching for information that was relevant, and formulating a broad concept of where the firm wanted to go. These sessions were the basis for the firm's decision to franchise, for example. One problem with the planning process was, according to the firm's administrative staff as well as the branch managers, that it did not tend to result in a set of specific goals and objectives for the firm, or a set of priorities to guide them in carrying out there overall efforts. The frequent complaint was that many of the plans that were originally made at the beginning of the planning year tend to become "bumped" by more immediate problems handed down by top management. The introduction of unplanned projects, or crises which tended to emerge, resulted in shifts in the focus of energy, and would result in neglect of many of the projects which had been originally agreed to at the beginning of the year. There was a sense that the firm was making progress, but that a great deal of the progress was in an ad hoc, or piece meal basis. The bottom line was that many of the participants in the planning process sessions expressed uncertainty about how the content of the meetings would be translated into action.

Although the overall planning process was extensive, there had never been a formal consideration of what the company's key result areas ought to be. Accordingly, although the branch managers and in turn installation technicians understood in general what their role was, there was not a specific set of key result areas for which they were held accountable. Similarly, there were not a specific set of goals or objectives for which they were held accountable.

Another problem with the firm's control system related to the nature of its objectives and goals. Although most of the firms objectives and goals were not measurable, a few were quantifiable. Another problem was that the level of performance expected was unrealistic. For example, the times which were available as "standard times" for installation were thought by all but a few of the most talented and experienced installation technicians to be unrealistic. As a result, many of the employees found the standards to be demoralizing. Moreover, the enforcement of the standard was relatively uneven. Some branch managers tended to stick to standards and to evaluate installation technicians negatively whenever their performance was below standard, which was quite frequently. Other branch managers, who recognized the standards were not wholly realistic, tended to ignore them.

One strength of the measurement system of the firm was that it was organized on a "responsibility accounting basis." This meant that the firm had good information concerning the profitability of each individual branch. At each branch, the company had institutionalized a monthly financial review of the data. The representative of the home office met with the branch manager and examined the monthly financial report. They also discussed issues involving branch performances on such key factors as market share. Within each branch, however, the process of performance review was relatively uneven. Other than examination of overall bottom line profitability, there did not tend to be a review of performance in key result areas which supported that profitability. Discussions of "problems" would occur as they emerged. There was no systematic attempt to identify the critical success factors of the branch, to measure the branches performance in each one of those factors, and to examine it in depth. With respect to performance appraisals of each employee, there was an uneven emphasis by the different branch managers on evaluation of their subordinates. While it was company policy that employees were to be reviewed based on their performance on a yearly basis, some individuals indicated that over two years had passed since their last review. They also reported that feedback on their performance ranged from some very specific, constructive criticisms, to more global assessments of their performance. Many individuals indicated that they were not really sure how they were being evaluated by their managers, or either whether they were valued or not valued by their managers. One stated, " well, I'm still here, so I must be doing okay."

At this stage of the firm's development there was not a well designed compensation program. The administration of compensation increases was on an ad hoc basis. Some individuals had not received a salary increase in more than two years. There were no specific guidelines for salary increases that would be allocated in relationship to different levels of performance, such as excellent performance, good performance, or satisfactory performance. Individuals reported that they did not have a clear idea as to how increases in their compensation would result based upon different levels of performance.

Improvements in the Control System

An analysis of our description of the control system at Superior Alarm in the last section indicates that there are a number of problems in the design of that system. There are problems both in the individual components of the control system, as well as in the overall integration of the system. In this section, we shall examine some of those problems and make suggestions about how they can be improved.

Goals and Objectives. As described in Chapter 3, objectives and goals are the output of the firm's planning system. The companies strategic planning system should result in a statement of its mission, its key result areas, its objectives, and goals. In the case of Superior Alarm, the planning system is not functioning as well as it needs to provide a foundation for an effective control system. The basic problem with the planning process at Superior Alarm is that it is not producing a well defined statement of key result areas. The key result areas are necessary to provide an overall focus for the branch manager, and in turn the installation technicians and the administrative assistants. Once the key result areas for each branch are identified and defined, then it is necessary to further improve the planning process at Superior Alarm by generating a set of objectives and relationships to each key result area. The next step is to generate goals which, by definition, are specific, measurable and time dated in relationship to each objective. These steps will help overcome the problems faced by branch managers, installation technicians, and administrative personnel. To help avoid the problem of setting unrealistic goals, the branch manager, installation technicians, and administrative personnel, should participate in the process of setting these goals. It is particularly important that great care be devoted to insuring that the goals are measurable, specific, and time dated. Otherwise, they did not provide and effective basis as a comparison with actual performance.

Measurement Systems. A measurement system permits a company to represent the performance of a branch or individual in quantitative terms. At a company such as Superior Alarm, the measurement system includes the accounting information system, sales management system, and other sources of information. Although there seems to be ample financial information to assist managers, there does not appear to be adequate source of financial information concerning performance in the branches.

The company will need to do an analysis of each of its key result areas in order to insure that measurements are available to assess performance on each of these key factors. The measurements do not all have to be in dollar terms. Some can be in monetary terms, other can be in non-monetary terms. Some measurements can even be what may be characterized as "go/no go" measurements. This means that a manager can do an informal rating of whether something has happened or not happened. For example we might be able to assess the level of customer service by the number of written complaints or letters of praise received. Ultimately, the home office might conduct a telephone sample of customers and have the interviewer generate a judgement as to whether the service provided was "satisfactory or unsatisfactory." By then tabulating the number of satisfactory versus unsatisfactory responses, we can generate a "measurement" of branch performance in this key result area.

Rewards. A significant problem with the firm's control system is the lack of linkage between objectives, goals, measurements and rewards. The firm's compensation system does not appear to be linked to its objectives and goals. Individuals do not perceive that they are rewarded based upon their ability to achieve goals and objectives. Since people do not perceive a clear linkage between goals and objectives and compensation, there is unlikely to be a great deal of "ownership" of the goals and objectives. People may very well be motivated, but the firm's reward system is not either enhancing or channeling their motivation directly toward the goals and objectives that the branch seeks to attain.

To improve its control system, the firm will have to do an analysis of its overall compensation system. To be effective the compensation system should ideally provide incentive for an individual to achieve the goals and objectives that the organization wants to attain. An increasing number of entrepreneurial firms are relying on compensation systems which have a significant component based upon incentive compensation. In such circumstances, people are generally provided a base salary which is relatively competitive, and then opportunities for substantial increases in compensation linked to the achievement of individual and company objective and goals. Wherever feasible, a company should attempt to tie incentive compensation to measurable factors. However, even where this is not feasible, if management can identify the key factors it wishes people to focus upon, and indicate how incentive compensation will be based upon those factors, it will result in enhanced motivation of performance.

CONCLUSION

The design and evaluation of organizational control systems is a complex and difficult process. Yet it is possible to design effective systems of control, ones which cause people to behave in ways which are consistent with organizational objectives.

The failure to properly design a control system can lead to major problems in an organization or even to organizational failure. Although the state of the art of organizational control theory requires further development, this monograph has presented the basic concepts, theory, and research findings relevant to an understanding of control systems as well as a conceptual framework to facilitate their design, evaluation, and improvement.

An effective organizational control system can be a great competitive advantage for an organization. It is an intangible asset. An ineffective control system can be a major competitive weakness, and can even contribute to an organization's failure to grow or even survive.

ENDNOTES

66. See Eric Flamholtz, <u>Human Resources Accounting</u>, (Jossey-Bass Publishers, Inc., 1985).
67. <u>Ibid</u>.

REFERENCES

Flamholtz, E. Human Resources Accounting, San Francisco, CA: Jossey-Bass Publishers, Inc., 1985.

BIBLIOGRAPHY

Acland, D., "The Effects of Behavioral Indicators on Investor Decisions: An Exploratory Study," Accounting, Organizations and Society 1, 2/3 (1976), pp. 133-142.

Alexander, J.A., "Adaptive Change in Corporate Control Practices", Academy of Management Journal, 1991, 34:2, 251-280.

Alexander, Michael O., "An Accountant's View of the Human Resource," The Personnel Administrator, November-December, 1971, pp. 9-13.

American Accounting Association, A statement of Basic Accounting Theory, Sarasota, FL: AAA, 1966.

Anthony, R.N. and Dearden, J., Management Control Systems, Sixth Edition, Homewood, IL: Richard D. Irwin, 1979.

Argryis, C. "The Dilemma of Implementing Controls: The Case of Managerial Accounting," Accounting, Organizations, and Society, 1990:15:6, 503-512.

Asch, S.E., "Studies of Independence and Conformity: A Minority on One Against a Unanimous Majority", Psychological Monographs, 70, whole no. 416 (1956).

Ashford, S.J. and A.S. Tsui, 1991,
"Self Regulation for Managerial Effectiveness: The Role of Active Feedback Seeking", Academy of Management Journal, 34: 251-280.

Auebach, Len R. and S. Sandan, "A Stochastic Model for Human Resources," California Management Review, Summer, 1974, pp. 24-31.

Bakke, E.W., "The Human Resources Function," Management International Review March-April, 1961, pp. 16-24.

Baron, Robert A., 1990,
"Countering the Effects of Destructive Criticism: The Relative Efficacy of Four Interventions", Journal of Applied Psychology, 75: 235-245.

Bass, B.M., Leadership and Performance Beyond Expectations, New York: Free Press, 1985.

Becker, Gary S., Human Capital, New York: National Bureau of Economic Research, 1964.

Bennis, W. On Becoming A Leader, Reading, Mass., Addison-Wesley, 1989.

Bennis, W. and Nanus, B., Leaders, New York: Harper & Row, 1985.

Berkshire, J.R. and R.W. Highland, "Forced Choice Performance Rating: A Methodological Study," Personnel Psychology, 6 (1963) pp. 355-378.

Bhambri, A., and H. Sonnenfeld, "Organization Structure and Corporate Social Performance: A Field Study in Two Contrasting Industries", Academy of Management Journal, 1988, 31:3, 642-662.

Birnberg, J.G. and Snodgrass, C., "Culture and Control: A Field Study," Accounting, Organizations and Society, Vol. 13, No. 5, 1988, pp. 447-464.

Bittner, R.H., "Developing an Industrial Merit Rating Procedure" Costello, Timothy W. and Sheldon S. Zalkind, Psychology in Administration, Prentice-Hall, Inc., Englewood Cliffs, N.J., 1963, p. 24.

Brownell, D., "Participation in the Budgeting Process - When It Works and When It Doesn't," Journal of Accounting Literature, Vol. 1, Spring 1982, pp. 124-153.

Brummet, R.L., E.G. Flamholtz and W.C. Pyle, "Human Resource Measurement - Challenge for Accountants," The Accounting Review, April, 1968, pp. 217-24.

Buckley, J.W. and K. Lightner, Essentials of Accounting, (Encino, CA: Dickenson Publishing Co., 1975).

Business Week Staff, "Why Griffiths is Out as RCA Chairman, Business Week, February 9, 1981, pp. 72-73.

Cammann, C., "The Impact of a Feedback System on Managerial Attitudes and Performance," Unpublished Ph.D. dissertation, Yale University, 1974.

Cammann, C., "Effects of the Use of Control Systems," Accounting, Organizations and Society, 1, 4, 1976, pp. 301-314.

Campbell, N.R., Foundations of Science, New York, NY: Dover Publications, 1957.

Capon, A.N., Christodoulou, C., Farley, J.U., and H.M. Hubert, "Comparative Analysis of the Strategy and Structure of U.S. and Australian Corporations, Journal of International Business Studies, 1987, 18:1, 51-74.

Carper, W. and J.M. Posey, "The Validity of Selected Surrogate Measures of Human Resource Value: A Field Study," Accounting, Organizations and Society, 1, 2/3 (1976), pp. 143-152.

Carroll, J.B., Language and Thought, Englewood Cliffs, NJ: Prentice-Hall, Inc., 1964.

Chatman, J.A., "Matching People and Organizations: Selection and Socialization in Public Accounting Firms", Administrative Sciences Quarterly, 1991, 36, 459-475.

Cherrington, D.J., "The Effects of a Central Incentive -- Motivational State on Measures of Job Satisfaction," Organizational Behavior and Human Performance, 1973, 10: pp. 271-289.

Cherrington, D.J., Reitz, H.J. an Scott, W.E., "Effects of Reward and Contingent Reinforcement on Satisfaction and Task Performance," Journal of Applied Psychology, 1971, 55: pp. 531-536.

Chesney, A.A. and E.A. Locke, 1991,
    "Relationships Among Goal Difficulty, Business Strategies, and Performance on a Complex Management Simulation Task", Academy of Management Journal, 34: 162-193.

Child, J., "Organizational Growth," in S. Kerr (Ed.), Organizational Behavior, Columbus, Ohio: Grid Publishing Co., Inc., 1979, Chapter 16, pp. 379-399.

Cleveland, J.N., Murphy, K.R., and R.E. Williams, "Multiple Uses of Performance Appraisal: Prevalence and Correlates", Journal of Applied Psychology, 1989, 74, 130-135.

Conger, J.A., "The Charismatic Leader," San Francisco, CA: Jossey-Bass, 1989.

Conlon, Edward.J. and Parks, J.M., "Effects of Monitoring and Tradition on Compensation Arrangements: An Experiment with Principal-Agent Dyads", Academy of Management Journal, 1990, 33, 603-633.

Connellan, Thomas K., "Management Development as a Capital Investment," Human Resource Management, Summer, 1972, pp. 2-14.

Covaleski, M. and M. Aiken, "Accounting and Theories of Organizations: Some

Preliminary Considerations", Accounting, Organizations and Society, 1991, 11:4/5, 297-320.

Cowherd, D.W. and D. I. Levine, "Product Quality and Pay Equity Between Lower-Level Employees and Top Management: An Investigation of Distributive Justice Theory", Administrative Sciences Quarterly, 1992, 37, 2, 302-321.

Daley, I., James, J., Sundem, G., Kondo, Y. "Attitudes Toward Final Control Systems in the United States and Japan", Journal of International Business Studies, 1985, 3:91-110.

Dent, J.F., "Accounting and Organizational Cultures: A Field Study of the Emergence of a New Organizational Reality, Accounting, Organizations and Society, 1991, 16:8, 705-732.

Dermer, J., "Control and Organizational Order", Accounting, Organizations and Society, 1988, 13:1; 25-36.

Earley, P.C., T. Connolly, and G. Ekegren, 1989, "Goals, Strategy Development, and Task Performance: Some Limits on the Efficacy of Goal Setting", Journal of Applied Psychology, 74: 24-33.

Earley, P.C., G.B. Northcraft, C. Lee, T.R. Lituchy, 1990, "The Impact of Process and Outcome Feedback on the Relation of Goal Setting to Task Performance", Academy of Management Journal, 33, 87-105.

Earley, P.C., P. Wojnaroski, and W. Prest, "Task Planning and Energy Expended: Exploration of How Goals Influence Performance", Journal of Applied Psychology, 72,1,107-114.

Egelhoff, W.G., Organizing the Multinational Enterprise: An Information-Processing Perspective, Cambridge, MA: Ballinger, 1988.

Eisenhardt, K.M., "Control: Organizational and Economic Approaches," Management Science, Vol. 31, 1985, pp. 134-149.

Eisenhardt, K.M. and C.B. Schoonhoven, "Organizational Growth: Linking Founding Team, Strategy, Environment, and Growth Among U.S. Semiconductor Ventures, 1978-1988", Administrative Science Quarterly, 1990, 35:504-525.

Elias, Nabil, "The Effects of Human Asset Statements on the Investment Decision: An Experiment, Empirical Studies in Accounting: Selected Studies, 1972, pp. 215-233.

Ellul, J., The Technological Society, New York: Alfred A. Knopf, 1964.

Erez, M., P.C. Earley, and C.L. Hulin, 1985, "Impact of Participation on Goal Acceptance and Performance: a Two-Step Model", Academy of Management Journal, 28: 50-66.

Etzioni, A., A Comparative Analysis of Complex Organizations, Glencoe, IL: Free Press, 1961.

Etzioni, A., "Organizational Control Structure," in March, J.G. (ed.) Handbook of Organizations, Rand McNally, Chicago, Ill., 1965.

Ezzamel, M. and M. Bourn, "The Role of Accounting Information Systems in an Organization Experiencing Financial Crisis," Accounting, Organizations and Society, 1990,26:5, 399-242.

Flamholtz, E.G.,"Accounting, Budgeting, and Control Systems in Their Organizational

Context: Theoretical and Empirical Perspectives", <u>Accounting, Organizations and Society</u>

Flamholtz, Eric, "The Theory and Measurement of an Individual's Value to an Organization," Unpublished PhD. dissertation, University of Michigan, 1969.

Flamholtz, Eric, "A Model for Human Resource Valuation: A Stochastic Process with Service Awards," <u>The Accounting Review</u>, April, 1971, pp. 253-267.

Flamholtz, Eric, "Assessing the Validity of a Theory of Human Resource Value: A Field Study," <u>Empirical Research in Accounting Selected Studies</u>, 1972, pp. 241-266.

Flamholtz, Eric, "Toward a Theory of Human Resource Value in Formal Organizations," <u>The Accounting Review</u>, October, 1972, pp. 666-678.

Flamholtz, Eric, "Human Resource Accounting: Measuring Positional Replacement Cost," <u>Human Resource Management</u>, Spring, 1973, pp. 8-16.

Flamholtz, Eric, "Assessing the Validity of Selected Surrogate Measures of Human Resource Value: A Field Study," <u>Personnel Review</u>, Summer, 1975, pp. 37-50.

Flamholtz, Eric, "Human Resource Accounting: A Review of Theory and Research," <u>Journal of Management Studies</u>, February, 1974, pp. 44-61.

Flamholtz, Eric, <u>Human Resource Accounting</u>, San Francisco, CA: Jossey-Bass Publishers, Inc., 1985.

Flamholtz, E.G., "Organizational Control Systems as a Managerial Tool," <u>California Management Review</u>, Vol. 22, No. 2, Winter 1979, pp. 50-59.

Flamholtz, E.G., "Toward A Psycho-Technical Systems Paradigm of Organizational Measurement," <u>Decision Sciences</u>, January 1979, pp. 71-84.

Flamholtz, E.G., <u>Growing Pains: How to Make the Transition from an Entrepreneurship to a Professionally Managed Firm</u>, San Francisco, CA: Jossey-Bass Publishers, Inc., 1990.

Flamholtz, Eric G., Jan B. Oliver and Robert Teague, "Subjective Information Valuation and Decision Making." Paper presented at the Western Regional AAA Meeting, Tempe, AZ, 1976.

Flamholtz, E.G., Das, T.K., and Tsui, A.S., "Toward an Integrative Framework of Organizational Control," <u>Accounting, Organizations and Society</u>, Vol. 10, No. 1, 1985, pp. 35-50.

Flamholtz, Eric and Todd S. Lundy, "Human Resource Accounting for CPA Firms," <u>CPA Journal</u>, XLV, October, 1975, pp. 45-51.

Fisher, Irving, <u>The Nature of Capital and Income</u>, London: Macmillan and Company, Ltd., 1927.

Fournet, G.P., M.K. Distefano, and M.W. Pryer, "Job Satisfaction: Issues and Problems." <u>Personnel Psychology</u>, Summer, 1966, p. 176.

Friedman, Abraham and Baruch Lev., "A Surrogate Measure for the Firm's Investment Human Resources" <u>Journal of Accounting Research</u>, 12, Autumn, 1974, pp. 23-250.

Gardner, W.R., "Attention: The Processing of Multiple Sources of Information," Handbook of Perception, Vol. II: <u>Psychophysical Judgement and Measurement</u>, Edited by E. Carterette and M. Friedman. New York: Academic Press, 1974, pp. 23-59.

Gellatly, I.R. and J.P. Meyer,"The Effects of Goal Difficulty on Physiological Arousal, Cognition, and Task Performance", Journal of Applied Psychology, 1992, 77:5,694-703.

Gerhart, B., and G.I. Milkovitch, "Organizational Differences in Managerial Compensation and Financial Performance", Academy of Management Journal, 1990, 33, 663-691.

Gerlinger, J.M. and Louis Hebert, "Measuring Performance in International Joint Ventures", Journal of International Business Studies, 1989, 22, 2, pp. 248-263.

Gerlinger, J. and Herbert L. "Control and Performance in International Joint Ventures", Journal of International Business Studies, 1990,2:235-254.

Glautier, M.W.E. and B. Underdown, "Problems and Prospects of Accounting for Human Assets," Management Accounting, March, 1973, pp. 98-102.

Gomez-Meija, L.R., Tosi, H., and T. Hinkin, "Managerial Control, Performance, and Executive Compensation, Academy of Management Journal, 1987, 30, 51-70.

Gordon, M.J., "Toward a Theory of Responsibility Accounting Systems," National Association of Accountants Bulletin, (December, 1973), pp. 3-9.

Govindarajan, V. and Gupta, A.K., "Linking Control Systems to Business Unit Strategy: Impact on Performance," Accounting, Organizations and Society, Vol. 10, No. 1, 1985, pp. 51-66.

Green, S.E. and M.A. Welsh, 1988,"Cybernetics and Dependence: Reframing the Control Concept", Academy of Management Review, 13, 287-301.

Grove, H.T., Mock, J. and Ehrenreich, K., "A Review of HRA Measurement Systems from a Measurement Theory Perspective," Accounting Organizations and Society, 1977, pp. 219-236.

Gupta, A.K. and Govindarajan, V., "Knowledge Flows and The Structure of Control Within Multinational Corporations," The Academy of Management Review, Vol. 16, No. 4, October, 1991, pp. 768-779.

Harder, J.W., "Play for Pay: Effects of Inequity in a Pay-For-Performance Context", Administrative Sciences Quarterly, 1992, 37, 2, 321-335.

Harpax, I., "Importance of Work Goals: An International Perspective," Journal of International Business Studies, 1990, 1:75-93.

Hedge, J.W. and M.J. Kavanagh, 1988,
"Improving the Accuracy of Performance Evaluations: Comparison of Three Methods of Performance Appraiser Training", Journal of Applied Psychology, 73: 68-73.

Hekimian, J.S. and Curtis H. Jones, "Put People on Your Balance Sheet," Harvard Business Review, January-February, 1967, pp. 105-113.

Hendricks, James, "The Impact of Human Resource Accounting Information on Stock Investment Decisions: An Empirical Study," The Accounting Review, LI, April, 1976, pp. 292-305.

Hermanson, Roger H., "Accounting for Human Assets." Occasional Paper No. 14, Bureau of Business and Economic Research, East Lansing, MI: Graduate School of Business Administration, Michigan State University, East Lansing, 1964.

Hirst, M.K., "Intrinsic Motivation as Influenced by Task Interdependence and Goal Setting", ??

Hofstede, G., "The Poverty of Management Control Philosophy," Academy of Management Review, July 1978, pp. 450-461.

Hofstede, G. B. Neuijen, D.D. Ohayv, and G. Sanders, "Measuring Organizational Cultures: A Qualitative and Quantitative Study across Twenty Cases", Administrative Science Quarterly, 1990, 35:286-305.

Hollenbeck, J.R. and H.J. Klein, "Goal Importance, Self-Focus and the Goal Setting Process", Journal of Applied Psychology,, 1990, 74:2,204-211.

Hollenbeck, J.R. and C.R. Williams, "Goal Commitment and the Goal Setting Process: Problems, Prospects, and Proposals for Future Research", Journal of Applied Psychology, 72:2, 204-211.

Hoskisson, R.E., "Multidivisional Structure and Performance: The Contingency of Diversification Strategy", Academy of Management Journal, 1987, 30:2, 625-644.

House, R.J., Shapiro, H.J. and Wahba, M.A., "Expectancy Theory as a Predictor of Work Behavior and Attitude: A Reevaluation of Empirical Evidence," Decision Sciences, 1974, 5: pp. 481-506.

Ijiri, Yuji, Theory of Accounting Measurement, Studies in Accounting, Research No. 10, Sarasota, FL: American Accounting Association, 1975.

Ivancevich, J., "Effects of Goal Setting on Performance and Job Satisfaction," Journal of Applied Psychology, 1976, pp. 605-612.

Ivancevich, J., "Different Goal Setting Treatments And their Effects on Performance and Job Satisfaction," Journal of Applied Psychology, 1977, pp. 406-419.

Jaggi, Bikki and Hon-Shiang Lau, "Toward a Model for Human Resource Valuation," The Accounting Review, XLIX, April, 1974, pp. 321-329.

Jones, C.S., "The Attitudes of Owner-Managers Towards Accounting Control Systems Following Management Buyout", Accounting, Organizations and Society, 1992, 17:2, 151-168.

Kacmar, K. Michele and Gerald R. Ferris, "Theoretical and Methodological Considerations in the Age-Job Satisfaction Relationship", Journal of Applied Psychology, 75:2, 201-207.

Katz, D. and Kahn, R.L., The Social Psychology of Organizations, New York: Wiley, 1966.

Keats, Barbara W. and Michael A. Hitt, "Causal Model of Linkages Among the Environmental Dimensions and Macro Organizational Characteristics," Academy of Management Journal, 1988,31: 570-598.

Kernan, M.C., and R.G. Lord, "Effects of Valence, Expectancies, and Goal-Performance Discrepancies in Single and Multiple Goal Environments", Journal of Applied Psychology, 1990, 75:2,194-203.

Kerr, J.L., "Diversification Strategies and Managerial Rewards: An Empirical Study", Academy of Management Journal, 1985, 28, 155-169.

Kerr, S., "On The Folly of Rewarding A, While Hoping For B," Academy of Management Journal, December, 1975, pp. 769-783.

Kim, J. and Hamner, W., "The Effects of Performance Feedback and Goal Setting on Productivity and Satisfaction in an Organizational Setting," Journal of Applied Psychology, 1976, pp. 48-57.

Klein, J.I., 1990, "Feasibility Theory: A Resource-Munificence Model of Work Motivation and Behavior", Academy of Management Review, 15: 646-665.

Kluckhohn, C., "The Study of Culture," in D. Lerner and H.D. Laswell (Eds.), The Policy Sciences, Stanford, CA: Stanford University Press, 1951, pp. 86-101.

Konrad, A.M. and J. Pfeffer, "Do You Get What You Deserve? Factors Affecting the Relationship Between Productivity and Pay", Administrative Sciences Quarterly, 1991, 35, 258-280.

Kotter, J.P., The Leadership Factor, New York: Free Press, 1988.

Kotter, J.P. and J.L Heskett, Corporate Culture and Performance, New York, Free Press, 1992.

Kozlowki, G. and M.L. Doherty, "Integration of Climate and Leadership: Examination of a Neglected Issue, Journal of Applied Psychology, 1989, 74:4, 546-553.

Kroeber, A.L. and Kluckhohn, C., Culture: A Critical Review of Concepts and Definitions, New York: Vintage Books, 1952.

Latham, G.P. and Yukl, G.A., "A Review of Research in The Application of Goal Setting in Organizations," Academy of Management Journal, 1975, pp. 824-845.

Laughlin, R. "Accounting Systems in Organizational Contexts: A Critical Theory". Accounting, Organizations and Society, 1987, 0.:5, 479-512.

Lawler, E.E., Motivation in Work Organizations, Belmont, Ca: Brooks/Cole, 1973.

Lawler, E.E., "Control Systems in Organizations," in Dunnette, M. (ed.), Handbook of Industrial and Organizational Psychology, Rand McNally, 1976.

Lawler, E.E. and Rhode, J.G., Information and Control in Organizations (Pacific Palisades, CA: Goodyear Publishing Co., 1976).

Lev, Baruch and Aba Schwartz, "On the Use of the Economic Concept of Human Capital in Financial Statements," The Accounting Review, XLVI, January, 1971, pp. 103-112.

Lewin, D. and Mitchell, D.J.B., "Appraisal and Reward," Chapter 7 of Human Resource Management: An Economic Approach, PWS - Kent/Wadsworth, forthcoming.

Likert, Rensis, The Human Organization: Its Management and Value, New York: McGraw-Hill, 1967.

Likert, R., D.G. Bowers and R.N. Norman, "How to Increase a Firm's Lead Time in Recognizing and Dealing with Problems of Managing its Human Organization," Michigan Business Review, January, 1969, pp. 12-17.

Liden, R.C., Mitchell, T.R., and C.E. Summer, "Top Level Management Priorities in Different Stages of the Organizational Life Cycle:, Academy of Management Journal, 1985, 28, 291-308.

Locke, E.A., "Towards a Theory of Task Motivation and Incentives," Organizational Behavior and Human Performance, 1968, pp. 157-189.

Locke, E.A., Shaw, K.M., Saari, L.M., and Latham, G., "Goal Setting and Task Performance: 1969-1980," Psychological Bulletin, Vol. 90, 1981, pp. 125-152.

Luckett, P.F. and M.K. Hirst, "The Impact of Feedback on Inter-Rater Agreement Insight in Performance Evaluation Decisions", Accounting, Organizations and Society, 1989, 14, 379-389.

McClelland, D.C., The Achieving Society, Van Nostrand, 1961.

McGowen, Peter, "Human Asset Accounting," Management Decision, Summer, 1968, pp. 86-89.

McLuhan, M., Understanding Media: The Extensions of Man, New York: McGraw-Hill Book Company, 1964.

Martinez, J.I. and Jarillo, J.C., "The Evolution of Research on Coordination Mechanisms in Multinational Corporations," Journal of International Business Studies, Vol. 20, 1989, pp. 489-514.

Maslow, Albert P., "Research Roundup," Personnel Administration, 31, No. 2 (March-April 1968), pp. 19-20.

Matsui, T., Kakuyama, T., and Ongatco, "Effects of Goals and Feedback on Performance in Groups", Journal of Applied Psychology, 1987, &2:3,407-415.

Merchant, K.A., Control in Business Organizations, Boston: Pitman Publishing, Inc., 1985.

Merchant, K. "The Effects of Financial Controls on Data Manipulation and Management Myopia", Accounting, Organizations and Society, 1990, 15:4, 297-314.

Meyer, J.P. and Gellatly, I.R., "Perceived Performance Norm as a Mediator in the Effect of Assigned Goal on Personal Goal and Task Performance", Journal of Applied Psychology, 1988, 73:3,410-420.

Micelli, M.P., Jung, I., Near, J.P.M. and Greenberger, D.B., "Predictors and Outcomes of Reactions to Pay-For-Performance Plans", Journal of Applied Psychology, 1990, 75, 2, 508-521 .

Miles, R.E., "Human Relations or Human Resources," Harvard Business Review, July-August, 1965, pp. 148-63.

Miller, Danny, Cornelia Droge, and Jean-Marie Toulouse, "Strategic Process and Content as Mediators Between Organizational Context and Structure", Academy of Management Journal, 1988,31:544-569.

Mintzberg, H., The Nature of Managerial Work, New York: Harper & Row, 1973.

Mirvis, P.H. and Lawler, E.E., "Measuring the Financial Impact of Employee Attitudes," Journal of Applied Psychology, Vol. 62, No. 2, 1977, pp. 1-8.

Mitchell, J.R., "Expectancy Models of Job Satisfaction, Occupational Preference and Effort: A Theoretical, Methodological, and Empirical Appraisal," Psychological Bulletin, 1974, 81: p. 1053-1077.

Mitchell, T.R. and W.S. Silver, "Individual and Group Goals When Workers Are Interdependent: Effects on Task Strategies and Performance", Journal of Applied Psychology, 1990, 75:2, 185-193.

Mock, T.J., Measurement and Accounting Information Criteria, Studies in Accounting, Research No. 13, Sarasota, FL: American Accounting Association, 1976.

Morse, Wayne, J., "A Note on the Relationship Between Human Assets and Human Capital," The Accounting Review, XLVIII, July, 1973, pp. 589-593.

Nahavandi, A. and A.R. Malekzadeh, "Acculturation in Mergers and Acquisitions", 1988, Academy of Management Review, 13: 79-90.

Norburn, D., Birley, S., Payne, A., and Dunn, M., "A Four Nation Study of the

Relationship between Marketing Effectiveness, Corporate Culture, Corporate Values and Market Orientation", Journal of International Business Studies, 1990, 3: 451-468.

Ogan, Pekin, "A Human Resource Value Model for Professional Service Organizations," The Accounting Review, LI, April, 1976, pp. 306-320.

Oliver, J. and E. Flamholtz, "Human Resource Replacement Cost Numbers, Cognitive Information Processing, and Personnel Decisions: A Laboratory Experiment," Journal of Business Finance and Accounting, Summer, 1978, pp. 137-158.

Oi, Walter, Y., "Labor as a Quasi-Fixed Factor," Journal of Political Economy, December, 1962, pp. 538-555.

Osborn, R.N. and C.C. Baughn, "Forms of Interorganizational Governance for Multinational Alliances", Academy of Management Journal, 1990, 33:2, 503-519.

Otley, D.T. and Berry, A.J., "Control, Organizations and Accounting," Accounting, Organizations and Society, 5, 2, pp. 231-244.

Ouchi, W.G., "The Relationship Between Organizational Structure and Organizational Control," Administrative Science Quarterly, Vol. 22, 1977, pp. 95-113.

Ouchi, W.G., "A Conceptual Framework for the Design of Organizational Control Mechanisms," Management Science, 1979, 25, pp. 833-847.

Ouchi, W., Theory Z, Addison-Wesley Publishing Company, 1981.

Ouchi, W.G. and McGujire, M., "Organizational Control: Two Functions," Administrative Science Quarterly, Vol. 20, 1975, pp. 559-569.

Parker, J.W., E.K. Taylor, R.S. Barrett and L. Martens, "Rating Scale Content: III. Relationship Between Supervisory- and Self-Ratings," Personnel Psychology, XII (1959), pp. 49-63.

Perrow, C., "The Bureaucratic Paradox: The Efficient Organization Centralizes in Order to Decentralize," Organizational Dynamics, 1977, pp. 3-14.

Peters, T.J. and Waterman Jr., R.H., In Search of Excellence, New York: Harper & Row, 1982.

Pierce, J.L. Stevenson. W.B., and James L. Perry, "Managerial Compensation Based on Organizational Performance: A Time Series Analysis of the Effects of Merit Pay", Academy of Management Journal, 1985, 28, 261-278.

Pond III, S.B. and P.D. Geyer, "Employee Age as a Moderator of the Relation Between Perceived Work Alternatives and Job Satisfaction", Journal of Applied Psychology, 72:4, 552-557.

Poole, M.S. and A.H. Van De Ven, "Using Paradox to Build Management and Organization Theories", Academy of Management Review, 1989, 14:562-568.

Prakash, P. and Rappaport, A., "Information Inductance and Its Significance for Accounting," Accounting, Organizations and Society, 1977, pp. 29-38.

Pyle, William C., "Monitoring Human Resources--On Line," Michigan Business Review, July, 1970, pp. 19-32.

Rosengren, W.R., "Structure, Policy and Style: Strategies of Organizational Control." Administrative Science Quarterly, Vol. 12, No. 1, June 1967, pp. 140-64.

Ross, I.C. and A. Zander, "Need Satisfactions and Employee Turnover," Personnel Psychology, Autumn, 1957, pp. 327-38.

Russell, J.A., and D.I. Goode, "An Analysis of Managers' Reactions to Their Own Performance Appraisal Feedback," Journal of Applied Psychology,1988, **73**, pp. 68-73.

Sackman, S.A., "Culture and Subcultures: An Analysis of Organizational Knowledge", Administrative Science Quarterly, 1992, 37: 140-161.

Sandelands, L.E., Brockner, J., Glynn, M.A., "If at First You Don't Succeed, Try, Try, Again: Effects of Persistence, Performance Contingencies, Ego Involvement and Self-Esteem on Task Persistence", 73:2,208-216.

Schacter, S.N., Ellertson, McBride, D. and Gregory, D., "An Experimental Study of Cohesiveness and Productivity," Human Relations, 1951, pp. 229-238.

Schmidt, F.I., Hunter, J.E., Outerbridge, A.N. and S. Gaff, "Joint Relation of Experience and Ability with Job Performance: Test of Three Hypotheses", Journal of Applied Psychology, 1988, **73**, pp. 56-67.

Schultz, Theodore W., "Investment in Human Capital," American Economic Review, 1961, pp. 1-17.

Schwan, E.S., "The Effects of Human Resource Accounting Data on Financial Decisions: An Empirical Test," Accounting, Organizations and Society, 1976, pp. 219-238.

Scott, W.G. and Mitchell, T.R., Organization Theory, Revised Edition, Homewood, IL: Richard D. Irwin, 1972.

Shalley, C.E. and G.R. Oldham, 1985, "Effects of Goal Difficulty and Expected External Evaluation on Intrinsic Motivation: A Laboratory Study", Academy of Management Journal: 28: 628-640.

Shalley, C.E., G.R. Oldham, and J.F. Porac, 1987, "Effects of Goal Difficulty, Goal-Setting Method, and Expected External Evaluation on Intrinsic Motivation", Academy of Management Journal: 30: 553-563.

Sheehy, G., Passages, New York: E.P. Dutton & Co., Inc., 1974.

Shenkar, O. and S. Ronen, "Structure and Importance of Work Goals Among Managers in the People's Republic of China", Academy of Management Journal, 1987, **30**:3, 564-576.

Shields, M.D., Birmberg, J.G. and Hanson Frieze, Il. "Attribution, Cognitive Processes and Control Systems," Accounting, Organizations and Society, Vol. 6, No. 1, 1981, pp. 69-93.

Shoorman, F.D., "Escalation Bias in Performance Appraisals: An Unintended Consequence of Supervisor in Hiring Decisions", Journal of Applied Psychology,1988, **73**, pp. 46-57

Sloan, A.P., My Years at General Motors. New York: MacFadden-Bartell, 1965.

Slovic, P. and S. Lichtenstein, "A Comparison of Bayesian and Regression Approaches to the Study of Information Processing in Judgment," Organizational Behavior and Human Performance, 1971, pp. 649-744.

Snell, Scott A., "Control Theory in Strategic Human Resource Management: The Mediating Effect of Administrative Information", The Academy of Management Journal, 1992, **35**, 2.

Staw, B.M., Intrinsic and Extrinsic Motivation, Morristown, M.J.: General Learning Press, 1976.

Stedry, A.C. and Kay, E., "The Effects of Goal Difficulty on Performance: A Field Experiment," Behavioral Science, 1966, pp. 459-470.

Stevens, S.S., "On The Theory of Scales of Measurement," Science, 1946, pp. 667-680.

Sullivan, J., 1988, "Three Roles of Language in Motivation Theory", Academy of Management Review, 13, 104-115.

Taylor, James E. and David G. Bowers, The Survey of Organizations, Ann Arbor, MI: Institute for Social Research, 1972.

Terborg, J., "The Motivational Components of Goal Setting," Journal of Applied Psychology, 1976, pp. 613-621.

Thomas, E.J. and Fink, C.F., "Effects of Group Size," Psychological Bulletin, 1963, pp. 371-384.

Thompson, J.D., Organizations In Action, New York: McGraw-Hill, 1967.

Thornton, George C., "The Relationship Between Supervisory- and Self-Appraisals of Executive Performance," Personnel Psychology, (1968), pp. 441-455.

Tomassini, L.A., "Assessing the Impact of Human Resource Accounting: An Experimental study of Managerial Decision Preferences," The Accounting Review, October, 1977, pp. 904-914.

Tosi, H.L. and Gomez-Meija, L., "The Decoupling of CEO Pay and Performance: An Agency Theory Perspective", Administrative Sciences Quarterly, 1989, 34, 2, 252-278.

Townsend, A.M., K.D. Scott, and S.E. Markham, "An Examination of Country and Culture-Based Differences in Compensation Practices", Journal of International Business Studies, 1990, 667-678.

Tsui, A.S., "A Multiple-Constituency Model of Effectiveness: An Empirical Examination at the Human Resource Subunit Level", Administrative Sciences Quarterly, 1990, 35, 458-490.

Tsurumi, Y., Japanese Business, Praeger Publishers, 1978.

Tsurumi, Y., The Japanese Are Coming, Ballinger Publishing Co., 1976.

Tubbs, M.E. and S.E. Ekeberg, 1991,"The Role of Intentions in Work Motivation: Implications for Goal-Setting Theory and Research", Academy of Management Review, 16: 188-199.

Vatter, William J., The Fund Theory of Accounting and Its Implications for Financial Reports, Chicago, IL: University of Chicago Press, 1947.

Vecchio, R.P., "Situational Leadership Theory: An Examination of a Prescriptive Theory," Journal of Applied Psychology, 1987, 72,3, 444-451.

Vance, R.J. and A. Colella, 1990,
"Effects of Two Types of Feedback on Goal Acceptance and Personal Goals, Journal of Applied Psychology, 75: 68-76.

Walsh, J. and J. Seward, "On the Efficiency of Internal and External Corporate Control Mechanisms", Academy of Management Review, 1990; 15:3, 421-458.

Weber, M., The Theory of Social and Economic Organization, (translated by

Henderson, A.M. and Parsons, T.), New York: Free Press, 1947.

Weiner, N., Cybernetics, Cambridge, MA: M.I.T. Press, 1948.

Weiner, Y., "Forms of Value Systems: A Focus on Organizational Effectiveness and Cultural Change and Maintenance", Academy of Management Review, 13: 534-545.

Weingart, L.R., "Impact of Group Goals, Task Component Complexity, Effort and Planning on Group Performance", Journal of Applied Psychology, 1992: 77:5 682-693.

Williams, J.J. and C.R. Hinings, "A Note on Matching Control System Implications and Organizational Characteristics: ZBB and MBO Revisited:, Accounting, Organizations and Society, 1988, pp 191-200.

Williams, M.L. and G.F. Dreher, "Compensation System Attributes and Applicant Pool Characteristics", Academy of Management Journal, 35, 1992.

Williamson, O.E., The Economic Institutions of Capitalism, New York: Free Press, 1985.

Woodruff, R.L., Jr., "Human Resource Accounting," Canadian Chartered Accountant, September, 1970, pp. 2-7.

Wright,P.M., "Operationalization of Goal Difficulty as a Moderator of the Goal Difficulty-Performance Relationship", Journal of Applied Psychology, 1990, 75:3, 227-234.

Yasai-Ardekani, Masoud, "Effects of Environmental Scarcity and Muniference on the Relationship of Context to Organizational Structure," Academy of Management Journal, 1989,32:131-156.

Zalesny, M.D., "Rater Confidence and Social Influence in Performance Appraisals", Journal of Applied Psychology, 1990, 75, 3, 274-289.

Zander, A. and Medow, H., "Individual and Group Levels of Aspiration," Human Relations, 1963, pp. 89-115.

Zaunbrecher, Hilary C., "The Impact of Human Resource Accounting on the Personnel Selection Process," Unpublished PhD. Dissertation, Louisiana State University, 1974.

Zenger, T.R., "Why Do Employers Only Reward Extreme Performance? Examining the Relationships Among Performance, Pay and Turnover", Administrative Sciences Quarterly, 1992, 37, 2, 198-219.

INDEX

Note: Page numbers in italics refer to figures; page numbers followed by t indicate tables.